MUSIC
MINISTRY &
MIRACLES

Trinity Television and Me

L. G. BRACKEN

MUSIC, MINISTRY AND MIRACLES
Copyright © 2013 by L. G. Bracken

Printed in Canada

ISBN: 978-1-4866-0166-0

Word Alive Press
131 Cordite Road, Winnipeg, MB R3W 1S1
www.wordalivepress.ca

Cataloguing in Publication may be obtained through Library and Archives Canada

To the Author and Finisher of my faith, my King Jesus - Praise God from Whom all Blessings flow!

To my wonderful husband, Warren — Thank you for being you.

To Becky, Peter, and David - Thanks for being my children and bringing Ryan, Michelle, and Samantha into the fold of our family and giving us Carter, Cassidy, Noah, and Maelle.

To Jim and Marion, our partners and colleagues in Power in Praise - The frequency of sound that we create goes beyond the natural into the supernatural realm of high praise to our King.

Contents

Acknowledgement

"Trust in the Lord with all your heart and lean not to your own understanding; in all your ways acknowledge Him and He shall direct your paths" (Proverbs 3:5-6, NKJV)

I could not point to any person other than the Lord, the true Director of Life. He really has led me to all the resources and people who have helped me in this project.

Thank you, Lord.

1. Introduction

Sometimes in order to look and move forward, one has to review and ponder the past. Looking back over the past thirty-five-plus years, I have to say a big "Wow!" God is so good. He's done some amazing things in and through Christian media ministry. My own personal experience with this ministry revolved around the relationship I was privileged to be part of for many years with Trinity Television, also known as New Day Ministries/NOW TV, or *My New Day* as it became known. My life has certainly been blessed by knowing the founders of Trinity Television's *It's a New Day*—Willard and Betty Thiessen. They are true and genuine servants of God. They have ministered to and encouraged me so much that I can hardly count the many ways my life has been impacted by these dear people.

My husband, Warren, and I first met Willard in the early 1970's. The church we were attending sponsored a series in the "Pairs and Spares" Bible study group we attended that examined the different view-points and doctrines of a variety of Christian denominations. Representatives of different denominations were invited to come and talk to us about their views. We heard a wide spectrum of opinions that ranged from a minister who denied the virgin birth of Christ, to representatives from the

Spirit filled, Charismatic Movement. The two representatives from the latter view were, to say the least, an experience in and of themselves. The one gentleman was a fairly quiet, gentle man named Harold. The other gentleman was very expressive and extremely outgoing, friendly, and dynamic. This man was none other than Mr. Willard Thiessen.

I cannot remember the actual content of what they shared with us; my most vivid memory is of the vivacious and joyful way in which they spoke about the Lord's Spirit moving in His church today. Yes, Willard did have hair back then— long hair to his shoulders! His laugh was just as boisterous and infectious as it is today. They talked about "speaking in tongues," but I do not remember feeling fearful, intimidated or pressured into having the experience myself. We were given information, but more than that, we were given a first hand, up close and personal encounter with human beings empowered by the unseen true and living God in the person of God the Holy Spirit. Our first meeting with these Spirit-filled and joyful men aroused a desire in us to hunger and thirst after righteousness, and to seek more of God's love and power for our lives.

The next time we encountered the Thiessens and Trinity Television Incorporated (TTI) was through posters that began showing up around Winnipeg. These posters were advertising the launch of a local Christian television program. They showed a smiling man and woman holding hands, their free hands lifted Heavenward against the background of the Winnipeg skyline. The year was 1976, and I was pregnant with our first child. I had been excited about motherhood and being at home. A Christian television program produced in Winnipeg seemed too good to be true! I was thrilled to think of the wonderful possibilities of being able to turn on the TV and get spiritual teaching right in my own home! The debut of the program was really exciting. I began viewing *It's a New Day* from its first day on air, as I had stopped working around the fifth month of my pregnancy. In the past, I had been thrilled to discover Christian programs produced in the United States and shown over our Canadian airwaves, but there was no comparison to the joy of having a locally produced and home-grown Canadian Christian witness on television.

2. This is the Day That the Lord Has Made. I Will Rejoice!

After our daughter was born in February of 1977, we decided to go into full time ministry with Youth for Christ. We were privileged to be interviewed on *It's a New Day* during that time. Warren says that I talked for most of the interview. I don't remember, because something happens to you when you are being interviewed on TV—your mind goes into automatic pilot, and time breezes by really, really quickly! We were with YFC for a year before Warren returned to work for the truss manufacturer he had been with prior to his stint with Youth for Christ.

We were also part of a contemporary Gospel group called Power in Praise. This group was one of the premier praise and worship groups in Manitoba. We had full time jobs in the secular work world and did our music ministry on the weekends and vacations. We really were living the best of all possible worlds, because we could go and bless people with our music and not worry about raising support to pay the bills. The Lord had given us the instruction that we were not professional. This didn't mean that we weren't proficient, but that He had other plans for our abilities.

We were able to enjoy our ministry without any financial burden. It was great! The ministry of Trinity Television became a place for us to be able to share our music ministry as well as our finances. We gave joyfully as we were able, just for the pure pleasure of knowing that we were sowing seeds of ministry into people's lives through the use of television. We sang on *It's a New Day* and joined with Trinity Television in producing an album called *I'm Coming Home, Lord*. All proceeds from the sale of that recording were directed back into the ministry of Trinity Television. We had the great joy of partnering with this groundbreaking and Christ centered ministry for the first five years of its influence in the Winnipeg marketplace. Knowing that we have been part of the Trinity ministry almost from its inception gives us a warm glow; we witnessed the Lord take the airwaves back for Christ. Other programs have been birthed with this same desire and passion to use media for the advancement of God's Kingdom. I am still amazed that a local program could grow to a nationwide and worldwide influence for our King Jesus. I am so glad that I have been personally used in different ways to support and help define this ministry.

As a musician, I have shared music; however, other areas of my creativity have been pressed into service, stretching me beyond my imagination. In 1985, the program coordinator was a young lady named Susan Michaels. She used to pick my brain for a lot of different ideas. Once she asked me for any ideas I might have for simple set design. I'm not a set designer by profession, but God gave me some inspiration, so I roughly sketched some ideas with columns and wispy drapery types of hangings to form an open concept "room" where musicians could stand. I say that I "roughly sketched" it because my "chicken scratch" was pretty elementary, but she seemed to get the idea of what I was trying to communicate. One day, I walked onto the set and, lo and behold, there they were—columns arranged in a semi-circle to form a "room" where the musicians could stand! How cool was that!

Susan challenged me to stretch my imagination and gifts in other areas. She wanted to have a musician's newsletter for the many people who contributed to the ambiance of *It's a New Day*. She asked me to write my thoughts about music ministry, since I had been around musically since the early 1970s. I recently found a letter I wrote to Susan in response to her request. The letter is dated September 9, 1985.

Dear Susan,
It feels a little strange, writing down my little bit of wisdom for the other musicians who have had the privilege of being on It's a New Day; *however, I suppose anything I share will be from my heart, and since Jesus is in there, I guess the wisdom won't be so little, after all.*

I am personally blessed every time I'm invited to come to the program and add to the musical segments, because it is exciting to see how the Lord fits the songs into the message of the day. I know this has happened time and again on the show, and it never ceases to amaze me how the Holy Spirit uses us, even without us trying to make everything fit. His ways are indeed higher than ours.

Sometimes, I feel like Manitoba's "grand old lady" of gospel music. This isn't because I'm that old, or that grand, but simply because Warren and I have been in gospel groups since 1970. I know there are people in Manitoba with much more background than that, but I'm speaking of the specific field of contemporary gospel. The first group we were involved with was composed of people in our youth group. There were four of us—three guys, and yours truly!

It's funny to think back on my first "solo". We were at a coffee house in Winnipeg, well practiced with about a half dozen songs. We were into the introduction for "Kumbya," and off I went, right on cue—alone. As a friend of ours once wrote , "she kept on singing, and has never looked back."

It's true that I have never let mistakes or bloopers make me fumble, even when the other members of the group missed their entrance. I guess the guys had some secret desire to just let me take the big step into the realm of lead singer. Since then, I have chuckled to myself over the lovely, yet naïve, beginnings of our singing ministry. I must say that the Lord probably has His share of chuckles at the offerings of His young children. Our earliest musical experiences participating in gospel concerts occurred mainly at coffee houses, banquets, church bazaars, and variety shows. Our motivation was based on the fact that we were a church youth group; therefore, we were supposed to sing at church functions purely as entertainment. Back then, I really didn't feel like we were worshipping; we were mainly becoming performers. The Lord didn't hit us over the head with our lack of spirituality; He just let us go and grow. Along the way, He brought people into our lives with the specific mission of teaching us that the Lord seeks those who will worship Him, in spirit and in truth.

We didn't become sensitive to the difference between Gospel singing and gospel singing right away. Allow me to clarify the difference between the two "gospels" (besides one having an uppercase G and the other a lowercase one.) First, gospel singing is the world's idea of the inspirational songs anyone can sing. There are lots of Christmas albums put out by secular artists whose lives are anything but Christ-like. There are also many people in show business who cut 'inspirational' records but are not followers of Jesus, nor do they pretend to be Christians. When we were in Nashville eighteen months ago, we were amazed at the attitude of some people regarding gospel music. It was lumped together with all the other kinds of music—no better or worse, not sacred or life changing. It was just another type of music to be used for business. Of course, not everyone who goes to Nashville to record a gospel album has this attitude, but that city is so saturated with all kinds of music that real gospel music just doesn't make an impact. In contrast to this, Gospel music focuses on worshipping the Lord in spirit and in truth. It tells about the life changing good news that Jesus Christ is the same yesterday, today, and forever. Gospel music allows the Holy Spirit to blow through us with His cleansing, healing breath, as it tells a dying world that there is life eternal through the finished sacrifice of Christ if they'll only repent of the thing that is killing them—sin. This music exhorts the Body of Christ to become the pure, spotless bride waiting for her bridegroom to come and take her home. This is the power of the Gospel, put to music for us to share.

I learn so much from the Lord, and my personal walk with Jesus is what has always given me the courage and confidence to go before the cameras, or walk onto a stage, or get up in front of a congregation in a church. His life in me is what makes it all joy. I can't receive praise for doing what is a privilege and an honor. His gift of music is one which must be given away, and then He multiplies the gift in so many diverse and wonderful ways beyond our comprehension. I'm not a singer because I have a voice that is able to hold a tune. I'm a singer because His song wells up within me, and I just have to let it out in order to fulfill the ministry that

God has called me to. It is only by His grace , salvation and the power of His Holy Spirit that I can do this.

Time and again I am in awe at the things the Lord says and does through me. I am as much a receiver of His blessings as are those who listen to the songs being sung. If I could give any encouragement to my brothers and sisters of like precious faith, it would be to let Jesus be your source in all things, for His well never runs dry. Let all you say and do be consistent in a life that seeks only to serve. Serve Jesus by being a servant to those around you; being in the limelight should only make you more aware of His presence.

That's it! I hope it is something you can use, and I hope you have been touched.
Linda Bracken

When I re-read that letter from so many years ago, I am amazed that I had such a deep understanding of the simplicity of the truth. I think that as I am becoming older my mind is finally catching up with what my spirit knew all along, and that the "new revelations" I am discovering today are really nuggets of gold that have been buried deep inside of me since the day I was born again.

Susan called me one day in December of 1985. Our dear friend, Jim Wimbush, had gone home to be with Jesus, and Susan was helping coordinate the funeral service. I had been singing a song for a few years that she said would be very appropriate for the service. I thought about the first time I had heard that special song and the effect it had had on me. In 1981 I was beginning to feel that my musical style and direction was supposed to change. Around that time I attended a Youth for Christ banquet in Portage La Prairie. The guest soloist for the evening performed standard contemporary Christian music, very similar to the style of music that I had been doing. At one point in her presentation, however, she sat at the piano and performed a style/variation medley of "Jesus Loves Me." She used different musical interpretations, from the slightly off-key voice of a very small child, to Barbra Streisand and Karen Carpenter impersonations, to a rousing, full operatic Maria Callas finish! She laughed at herself as a ham, and then she led us in singing that sweet, simple song with her. When we had finished, she stood up and performed a song that resonated in my spirit. The song built up to a crescendo of praise and adoration and worship before our King Jesus. The musical image of seeing Jesus face to face, along with the Christian hope of the resurrection from the dead, was exhilarating! It was as if I was caught up to God's throne room in the spirit. God put a desire in my heart to worship Him with that kind of pure, unadulterated, unbridled fervor. The singer was Sandi Helvering (also known as Sandi Patty), and the song was "We Shall Behold Him." Death no longer has a sting, and the message of hope sends healing into hearts broken by sorrow.

When I stand in the powerful flow of music that is anointed and breathed by the Holy Spirit, I ache in my heart to see this powerful tool used for its original purpose of bringing honor and glory to our worthy Creator. The sad truth is that some of the folks in the Christian music business have fallen away from their first love and been seduced by the lure of the money, power and prestige of being in the limelight. I hope and pray that as the singers and songwriters of the next generation are exposed to the opportunity to be used in this powerful, visible medium, they will cling to the Lord and rely on His Word to sustain, challenge, and motivate them. Okay, end of sermon! I can't help but be a little protective when I see the great potential that the Gospel in musical form can have to speak to people's deep need to know the Lord.

On the day of Jim's funeral, I really wanted to let God flow through me. I prayed that I would not become emotional to the point of not being able to sing, but God was faithful and poured through me in a powerful way. I knew it was God singing into the hearts of the people. He was singing His song of truth and love and hope; I was simply the delivery system for His message. I felt that same flow of God through me whenever I was obedient to His leading regarding the musical selections for *It's a New Day*. There were times when the power of the Lord would be tangible in the studio.

One day I had been directed by the Lord to do the song "Wounded Soldier," which speaks of the sacrifice of those who, in the course of working in the harvest field of the Lord, are buffeted by the evil one almost to the point of dying. Sometimes they are tripped up by the insidious temptations and traps set by the enemy. The mandate for the Body of Christ is to comfort those wounded ones with the oil of the Spirit and bind their hurts with God's love. Unfortunately, Christians are notorious for shooting their wounded. As I finished singing, there was a sort of "holy hush" in the studio. The guest for the day, John Sandford, was weeping. God's love was like a warm blanket around us; you almost didn't want to move or breathe. It was a still and sacred moment. There were many such moments during my time at Trinity Television, some televised and some not.

Keeping with the theme of wounded soldiers in the Body of Christ, I will fast forward in my narrative to the time when our friend, Audrey Meisner, admitted that she had committed adultery. During that time we did not know what was happening, as Bob and Audrey's private pain was not exposed to prying eyes. We were told that they were going to leave the ministry and go south of the border to a new calling. In hindsight, I think the situation was handled with tact and sensitivity by the

Thiessen family. What the enemy meant for evil, God turned around and used for good. God's people were in place to cover Bob and Audrey and their family with prayer, counsel and love.

Although we were not aware of what had taken place in the Meisner's lives, we knew something was going on that had far reaching consequences. Their story has been chronicled in their own books, and I am so glad that God still covers His wounded warriors—even when the wounds are self-inflicted. We have all sinned and come short of the glory of God. Many people wanted to condemn Audrey and disqualify her from God's ministry. Thank God that He does not hold our sins against us when we repent and choose His forgiveness. The Meisner's marriage was not only saved and restored, but they are using their story to bring hope and healing to others as they fight for the family unit and carry on the vision of *My New Day*. God sees us in our frailty and still uses us.

When *It's a New Day* was telecast from the studios of CKND, I would arrive about a half an hour before the program aired to practice with the sound crew. It was always a great way to fill the studio with God's music and welcome His presence. As I stood in the empty room and lifted my voice before Father's throne, I would forget that there were people in the production room listening in on my "royal command performance." One day I was practicing the lovely hymn, "Turn Your Eyes Upon Jesus." I had my eyes closed and I was singing for my Jesus. When the song ended I opened my eyes and saw one of the CKND news anchor people standing in the shadows. With tears in his eyes he simply said, "that was beautiful." I praised the Lord that He had faithfully used this vessel to sing His song into the heart of a seeker. I have been given so many opportunities to grow in my understanding of what God wants for us as His children. I know that I have not arrived at a full understanding, by any stretch of the imagination, but as one *It's a New Day* guest stated: "I have not arrived, but I'm on the train and I've left the station!"

I have to admit to you, there have been times when I have been less than gracious in my attitude, but God knows how to correct me without too much pain, as long as I learn my lesson quickly enough! One occasion of "attitude adjustment from the Lord" occurred on a telethon night when Susan had asked me to come in and sing. I got all ready to go. Externally, I had the right clothes and hair and makeup for singing on television, but internally, I had let some ego issues slip into the mix. You can fool all kinds of people, but you can never fool the Lord. He sees our hearts, motives, and attitudes with crystal clarity. I had to learn a lesson that night about who was really getting the glory through the ministry of music, and about the powerful atmosphere that we can project either for the kingdom of light or the kingdom of darkness!

Warren and I walked into the building on St. Anne's Road. Actually, Warren walked in and I swept in all "diva-like" with my background tape in hand! I was feeling very comfortable and self-assured; after all, I was used to this life of being on television, and I had the attitude of "let the bells ring out, let the banners fly, I know it's too good to be true, but I'm here...I'M HERE!"

Okay, maybe it wasn't that obvious, but Father God knew I had to be taken down a notch or two and reminded about what I was doing there and why I had been called to have the privilege of singing for my friend, Jesus. He knows exactly how to deal with us when we start "sportin' a 'tude!" The scriptures say, *"Pride goes before destruction, and a haughty spirit before a fall."* (Proverbs 16:18) Subtle are the ways of the enemy's lies.

As I floated into Trinity and offered my tape to the production people, I discovered that there had been some miscommunication and that I was not on the roster for music during the telethon! My external reaction was very understanding. I graciously offered to do whatever little job they wanted done. Little did I know that lurking in the shadows of my ego was a bit of a chip on my shoulder, a corner of resentment, a put out and spoiled little girl who was quietly pouting and sulking! God was watching my internal reaction with great interest. They suggested that I could go into the prayer room with the intercessors. No lights, no cameras, no center stage! On the outside everyone saw this compliant, self-effacing, gracious facade—but on the inside God was seeing the ugliness of disappointment and a bruised ego.

The praise and worship and prayer was in full swing as the crowd of intercessors clapped and sang fervently before the Lord! I went into the prayer room, and I was full of dark bitterness. On the outside I looked like I was into the singing and clapping, but anger and disappointment were boiling under the surface. God let me go a little while longer and then He said "Enough!" The worship leader stopped the music and said, "I don't know what it is, but there is a wall up that is preventing the flow of God's Spirit. It's as if there is an oppression that is stopping the prayers from being effective!"

When God lowers the boom, He means business and He doesn't mince His words. I knew that I was the culprit. I quietly repented before the Lord and asked Him to forgive me and set my heart right. The worship continued, and I felt the flow of God's love as He wrapped His arms around me and said into my heart, "You're forgiven."

The worship leader spoke out with joy and said that whatever the hindrance had been, it was gone! Praise the Lord! I thanked my Heavenly Father for forgiving me and setting me straight. The flow of the Lord's Spirit brought light and life into the intercession room. I was flying in the Spirit as I thanked my Lord Jesus with my hands uplifted in surrender to Him.

With tears of relief flowing down my face, I was enjoying the warm fellowship of my brothers and sisters as we basked in the glow of the Holy Spirit. Suddenly there was a movement behind me and I felt a light touch on my shoulder. It was the Thiessens' administrative assistant, Diane Lear, and she whispered in my ear that they had scheduled me to do my song during the telethon after all. Surprisingly, I did not want to leave the prayer room. I was actually disappointed that I couldn't stay in the prayer meeting and continue feeling the sweet presence of God's love! I was amazed that I felt such a difference in my attitude, and I realized how sneaky the enemy's lies are and how quickly we can fall into the trap of seeing ourselves as "stars." The focus should always be on the Lord of Glory! I am so grateful that He can see the deepest crevasses in our being and deal with us with justice and mercy.

On another occasion I was not obedient to God's instruction and argued with Him about doing what He asked me to do. I had arrived at Trinity Television's Christian Center on Chevrier Blvd. at 9:30 in the morning to get ready for *It's a New Day*. I gave my music tapes to the sound man and went to the studio to practice. Usually I would have a good idea of what the Lord wanted me to sing on a particular day, but on this day I had the impression I was to do a certain song that I had not practiced for a while. My fear was that I would not remember the song well enough to do it on television. I had the song in the car in my large tape case, but I felt that it was too late to go and retrieve it. I did my first musical selection, but God kept nudging me to go and get the other tape. I did not obey the Lord's impression, and the song that I should have done, but didn't, would have confirmed that day's guest's teaching. I wish I could say that I learned my lesson from that incident, but I am certainly a work in progress and God is still workin' on me.

I could relate more of my failures and triumphs, but I think I have given you the right idea that we are all walking on the road of faith. The faith walk that we are taking is an interesting journey with a wonderful destination, but until the day dawns and we enter our eternal rest, we get to choose every day how we should live.

I have such rich memories of those early years of partnership with Willard and Betty and being part of the *It's a New Day* team. As I stated in the letter from 1985, I was amazed and blessed at how many times the music that I chose (by God's direction and inspiration) fit with the topic of the day or the testimony of the person sharing. I should have stopped being surprised, but I was in awe every time I was obedient and God showed up. There were those other times when I was not obedient and eventually felt so bad that I had missed the mark, but God is a fair boss and doesn't fire us for blowing it. He just gives us another chance to learn from our mistakes and move on. He is so very good to me! I am so thankful that in spite of our failings and frailty, we are used in the kingdom for God's purposes. None of us are perfect, and we are all a work in progress.

One example of human frailty and our propensity to stumble involves the "gold tooth" story and Willard Thiessen. Willard had forgotten that his brother, a dentist, had given him a gold implant. A guest on the program had spoken healing words into the viewing audience that God was putting gold teeth in place. The guest looked at Willard's gold tooth and stated that a miracle had occurred in Willard's mouth! Willard was caught up in the excitement and really thought he had been the recipient of a miraculous gift from Heaven. The secular media went after our brother with a vengeance when Willard admitted his lapse in memory and admitted his dentist had given him the gold tooth. Once again, we are reminded that we are prone to missteps and mistakes. When we err and repent, God forgives and forgets. The finger pointers have their own issues to deal with; we forgive others, and ourselves, and move on in a new awareness of the gift of amazing grace.

3. Not Coincidence But "Godincidence"

As I share the different aspects of my time with TTI, I have to mention some of the people who have been put in my life who have a TTI connection. The first people are from my childhood.

When I was in elementary school, I was part of a little musical called *Top O' The World*. The character I played was a granny-from-the-*Beverly Hillbillies*-type of lady by the name of Ma Spinks. She was supposed to be a feisty and no nonsense lady who sang off key. The singing coach in charge of my training thought it best if I didn't learn how to sing off key. She reasoned that I would be harmed by being taught to sing flat, so she helped me sing on key. This lady, Mrs. Anita Kroeker, was married to the gentleman who directed the choir at my mother's church, Mr. Bert Kroeker. His cousin was Elizabeth Kroeker, who became Betty Thiessen. Betty and Bert's family owned a potato and vegetable farm. One of several companies my Father worked for in his career as a sales representative was Old Dutch Foods. He might have conducted business dealings with Don and Walter Kroeker, Betty's brothers.

Diane Lear, the Thiessen's administrative assistant, and her husband, Don, were good friends with my parents and my dad's brother. The Lears had known me since I was a small child, and I used to call them Uncle Don and Auntie Diane. How Diane became Willard and Betty's administrative assistant is what I call a "Godincidence."

After working for Old Dutch Foods, my dad was employed by CKY TV. One person who worked with my Dad there was a gentleman by the name of Mr. Al Koniuk. While watching *It's a New Day*, Al was challenged to give his life to the Lord Jesus. He became a follower of Jesus and received much spiritual nurturing from the daily program's teaching. Later on, Al was instrumental in initiating the CRTC application process on Trinity Television's behalf and in mentoring the fledgling production staff in the fine art of television production.

I have other people in my life who are interconnected through a variety of situations and relationships apart from Trinity Television. It's as if God needs to give me these "neon signs" to let me know He is in charge of our lives So often I stand in awe of how big God's plans are for us. He never leaves us without evidence that He is in control. How awesome and caring and personal is our dear Lord and Savior—Jesus!

I know that my relationship with Trinity Television has been designed and planned from the day of my conception. Every step of my life, whether I was aware of it or not, has been directed by the Great Director. I am humbled and awed and so privileged to be in His care. I only share these coincidences because they are all too perfectly planned out to be just a chance set of circumstances. I firmly believe in the Creator of the universe, and I know that you cannot have a design without a designer. I fully appreciate the miracle working power of our Lord in the everyday things that we enjoy on a constant basis. I think He takes great delight in seeing us become ecstatically excited about His purposes and plans.

I don't know about you, but I'm lovin' the adventure! I just hope that I don't become complacent about God, like the children of Israel did. These people were delivered from slavery in Egypt, they walked through the Red Sea and saw their enemies drown in the very waters that had opened up to allow them to escape, and they had God Himself lead them by a pillar of fire at night and a huge cloud during the day. Even so, they complained about the manna that God sent every day. How can you get bored with "angel's food"? We need to be careful that we don't lose our sense of awe over walking in the kingdom of our God. We need to be grateful every day for the daily provision of the Lord in our lives, both in the large and spectacular events as well as in the small, quiet, commonplace occurrences. Let our daily prayer be *"help me, Lord, to keep my child-like awe of who you are and what you do in my life every day, and help me keep a heart of gratitude for your many blessings! Amen and Amen."*

I will share a little later about some really huge faith building experiences that I have enjoyed specifically with my friends from Trinity Television. You will see how I have been challenged to look for the Lord's hand in many situations and circumstances of my life. There is so much that is not just a coincidence—it's a "Godincidence"! "Godincidence" refers to the perfect co-ordination of events and people to reveal the sovereignty of God in all the details of our lives. He is so good to us all the time, whether we recognize His moving in our lives or not. Sometimes we think about someone and go to phone them, only to have the phone ring first with that same person on the other end. Sometimes those times are not coincidences, but "Godincidences," the dovetailing of events for our good.

4. *It's a New Day*'s Personal Impact

Part of what I have to share about my experience with Trinity Television has to do with those times when God spoke to me personally and profoundly through the guests. Some guests were used as I watched the program in my home, while others spoke to my heart when I was in the studio as part of the team.

In the first season, a couple from Australia, Cliff and Helen Beard, appeared on the show. I loved listening to them. Maybe it was their "down under" accents, but I'm more inclined to think it was the deeply moving way they talked about the Lord. I was listening to them quite intently, and was actually hunched forward, straining to catch everything they were saying. At one point Helen turned to the camera and said, "There is a lady listening to the program today; you are listening so intently that you are hunched forward and listening. God sees you and He has a special plan for you."

I was so excited that God could see me, God knew who I was, and He cared enough about me as I sat in my living room to share through this lady on the television that He had something special planned for my life! That was the first time in my life that I knew that I knew that I knew that God really, really, really loves and knows me on a personal and intimate level. Everything I thought I knew about God up to that time paled in the realization of that moment. An obedient servant of the Lord spoke a word of knowledge just for me.

On another occasion I was sharing in song on the program. The topic of the day dealt with abortion, and it was one of those rare times when I knew ahead of time what the program's content was going to entail. I had chosen the music with care, knowing what a sensitive and painful subject was being presented to the audience. The song I chose was titled "Killing Thousands," an Annie Herring composition. I knew that God would powerfully speak to someone's inner hurt and need for healing and reconciliation. Little did I know that God would put His searchlight on my heart! The time was right for God to do some pruning in my life. I had been given information about someone I knew quite well who had chosen to end an unwanted pregnancy. I was heartsick for that person and grieved the loss of the innocent life and all of the potential that was thrown away by aborting that child. I felt that I was to minister the truth about the forgiveness and healing from the Lord for the many who had chosen to go down that path. Little did I know that I needed healing from a particular situation from my past.

When I was a small child I was exposed to inappropriate sexual handling by several people. Some were relatives, some were strangers. The one that affected me the most occurred with a relative when I was less than five years old. The memory of being involved in his immature sexual exploits left me feeling dirty and bad. I was too young to comprehend what had happened to me in the basement of my relatives' home, and back then people did not really talk about this sort of abuse.

After I received healing through the events that I am about to share, I corresponded with this person and told him of my forgiveness toward him because of God's love and forgiveness. I also wanted to let him know that I would be making this a part of my personal testimony, and that I would be sharing it publicly so that others could receive the hope of healing from their own experiences of abuse. When I met this relative a few years later at a family function, we were able to have a heartfelt time of reconciliation. I can truly say that I have no trace of residual bitterness toward this man.

On the particular day that I was part of the abortion topic program, the guest speaker at the end of the program said something along the lines of: "There is someone listening today who was abused and never really forgave their abuser. They are still in bondage to that abuse and today God wants to set them free!" At that moment it felt as though God gently put His hand on me and whispered, "Linda, it's you." That was it. I knew it was me. I knew that I had let that experience of abuse sit inside of me, and I had allowed the hurt to fester deep inside my heart. God knew what was hiding there, and in His perfect time He wanted to clean house.

I had thought that when I accepted the Lord Jesus all the deep, dark secrets of the past had been washed away. Yes, my Spirit had been made clean and given eternal life when I asked the Lord into my heart, but there were some areas of my mind, will and emotions that needed to be healed and redeemed. I have learned that true forgiveness requires more than just giving mental assent to the pain and recognizing the power of forgiveness. One must also acknowledge the need for reconciliation between the offender and the victim, and the words have to be spoken out loud so that the painful memory of the offense can be brought into the light, its bondage broken, and the effect of the enemy's lies nullified.

The scripture says, *"Now is the day of salvation"* (2 Corinthians 6:2), so after the program I told Betty that the speaker had been speaking about me. I briefly explained what had happened to me as a young child. She reassured me that I had done nothing wrong and that I was the victim. That was so good to hear, because I had always felt like I had done something bad and that I was to blame. As we walked into the prayer room, I felt the awful oppression of fear sweep over me. I sat down in the chair and could not shake the cold, awful dread that forced its way onto my head and shoulders. I could not speak, and I felt frozen. Betty told me that when she turned from closing the door she could feel the dark heaviness in the room. She came behind me and lightly put her hands on my head.

I knew I was supposed to forgive and say the words out loud, and I fought with everything I had to begin the process. Suddenly, I felt as though a dam broke inside and I was able to speak the words. The healing flow of forgiveness was so clean and pure and life giving! Betty told me later that once I released the words and the tears, she felt the darkness and oppression leave and the light of God's presence fill the room. I spoke the healing words, and I was truly set free from the chains of shame, past hurt, and unreleased words of forgiveness that had formed to try and keep me from really going forward in my Christian walk.

That day remains crystal clear in my memory; it's one of the shining moments I can think back on and rejoice over with thanksgiving because of the delivering power of the Lord of Glory. I have shared that part of my personal testimony in many venues, as well as on *It's a New Day*. I know that shining the light of God's truth on the deepest wounds can set the captives free, and whom the Son sets free, is free indeed! My hope is that someone reading or hearing my testimony will come to the Lord Jesus for healing. He is the only one who can bring freedom and liberty from the hurts and wounds of our life. The secret to freedom is really no secret at all. It just takes an act of faith to speak the words of forgiveness and receive by faith the Lord's personal and healing touch. Jesus says in the book of Revelation:

Behold, I stand at the door and knock. If anyone hears my voice and opens the door, I will come in to him and eat with him, and he with me. (Revelation 3:20)

In this passage of scripture, Jesus is speaking to the church at Laodicea about the doors of their hearts, but He is knocking on the doors of all of our hearts. When Jesus comes into the house of your life, He wants to help you clean house, not just stay in the foyer or in the dining room. He loves to clean out closets (your heart and soul), old cluttered attics (your past painful memories), and your basement (the deep hidden things of your heart). He takes care of the whole house, and by His stripes we are healed!

I have included the illustration above as an example of the analogies and life lessons I learned watching the many teachers who were guests on *It's a New Day*. There are so many excellent teachers and teachings available to the Body of Christ through ministries like Trinity Television that it is sometimes tempting to buy every book, tape, and video that is offered! I need to be careful, because I am a Christian resource junkie! There, I've said it. I'm hooked on the Word and the rich wealth of testimonials and teachings available to us. I'm like the proverbial kid in a candy store when it comes to the stupendous volume of Christian literature and music. I was always so thankful for Trinity's book club and video library. The only obstacle to my purchasing more than I did was my limited funds. After all, one does have to put food on the table and pay the electric bill (sigh)! I was thankful, however, for the little bit that I was able to access in the form of audio tapes, videos, and books.

I liked the fact that buying these life impacting materials from Trinity helped to undergird their ministry and support their efforts in a tangible way, as well as allowing me to access great spiritual teachings any time of the day or night in my own home or car. I also loved to give materials away to bless others for birthdays and Christmas and "just because" events, like getting together for coffee! I can honestly say that I have received so much from watching *It's a New Day* and being involved directly with the ministry that I can't begin to think of how much I owe them for their faithfulness in serving as a conduit for the Lord to pour through into the viewer's heart. I know that I am richer in spirit for having access to such wonderful and anointed programs.

God even used the program to speak healing to my heart through the very people who had been a cause of turmoil and distress. It happened just around the time of Trinity Television's Fifth Anniversary Banquet. We were attending a small Full Gospel Church at the time. The leadership had received notice that a Christian drama group from the United States would be in the area and would like to come and share with our congregation. They needed to be billeted in homes for the duration of their stay. We volunteered because we loved to help out with ministry. Little did I know what life in the spirit lessons I was going to be taught during the course of this three week visitation.

The troupe of actors came to town and performed at the church. After the evening service a newlywed couple, who were also on their honeymoon, and a single guy and gal came home with us. We wanted to be accommodating and generous in our hospitality, because we knew that would bless the Lord. We had always had positive and uplifting experiences in the past when we had been open to the Lord using our home, so we had no fear or apprehension allowing these people to share our space. I won't go into much detail about the time we had them living in our house, but they took advantage of us in numerous ways. For example, the newlyweds would disappear into the guest room and then reappear a while later looking for something to eat!

We should have clued in to the fact that our hospitality was being abused and that we were being manipulated and controlled, but we were naive and trusting. One of the things that we found out later was that the team would do improvisations as they were conversing with their hosts. This meant that we were being used to "act" with them, except we were not given that information, so we were not in on the "act." In other words, they remained in "acting mode" and were not themselves. We were unaware and deceived. I think what they were doing was feeling us out for how they could use us. We innocently allowed these people to be part of our family and ministry. We invited them to participate with their drama during a Power in Praise concert, and we invited them to Trinity Television's Fifth Anniversary Banquet.

The single girl, Bernice (not her real name), was especially manipulative. She recognized that I had a soft heart for people and that I wanted to be helpful. She and I would talk late into the night. She would act depressed and in need of counsel and comfort, and I would encourage her to let the Lord have full control in her life. We would pray, and she would act like she had had a major victory. The next morning, she would be depressed again and I would have to start encouraging and building her confidence again.

This pattern continued for quite a few days, and I was getting worn out from the late nights and the emotional demands. Bernice was taking so much of my time that I was neglecting the house, the kids, and Warren. Because it was the busy time of year in our company, Warren could not take the time to see what was happening. He became frustrated, but he did not step in to stop the "counseling sessions."

Eventually everything came to a devastating head at the Trinity Television Fifth Anniversary Banquet. Bernice had come to another "victory," and I really felt that I had helped her break through the depression and poor self-image. As we sat at the dinner table, she leaned over to me and said something that I don't remember, because the Lord has helped me to forget. I do know that the old pattern had returned, and she was letting me know that she was not happy and was not enjoying herself and was not helped. I could not take it one more minute. I really do not know how I reacted; I felt as if I was being pulled down a huge vortex that was swirling underneath me. As this was happening, I saw Jim, Mar and Warren. I just clung to them as I cried and said, "I really need you guys!" Bernice had disappeared at this point, so I was left alone with my shameful breakdown. At one point a dear friend of ours, Donna, came up to me and put her arms around me and hugged me tightly. I felt as if God had wrapped me in His great big embrace. Donna is a diminutive lady who stands less than five feet tall, but she is a giant in God's family!

I really don't remember much of the rest of the evening. I felt like a dish rag—all wrung out and weak. We drove home, and as I lay on the back seat of the car, Bernice said she felt bad and put her hand over the seat to hold my hand. I have since learned that this type of behavior is common in abusive, controlling people. They will drive you to the limit of yourself, then try to be your comforter. It is a sinister, insidious, and vile deception of behavior—manipulation and control for one's own purposes.

The next day, the newlywed man and the single man were interviewed on *It's a New Day*. I watched the program, and God actually spoke through those guys to me. I was crying and emotional, but God did a quick work of restoration in my heart and mind. Needless to say, the troupe was moved out of our house.

Bernice was put up in another home, and I knew that God had restored me and made me stronger in Him when I got a phone call from Bernice a few days later. She said, "Linda, I want to kill myself. I just want to die!" I held the phone for a few seconds, praying silently, and then in a rush God poured words out of me that were shocking, astounding, and filled with boldness that only came from above. I said, "Okay, go ahead and kill yourself!" Then I paused before I continued. "But you better do it right—lay down at the foot of the Cross and DIE!" There was absolute silence at the end of the phone. I didn't care if she took my advice or not, because I was not under her control and manipulation any more.

Bernice did not kill herself, but I don't know if she ever let Jesus really take control of her life. The most wonderful day arrived when we put her on the airplane. I still don't know why we got to take her to the plane, but it was an amazing relief! The story has one more facet to it. Years later I received a phone call from Bernice. She babbled on about being in Kansas with a travelling group of actors, and once I was able to get a word in edgewise, I told her that the wheat field behind us was golden and ready for harvest. I started to tell her that I felt the world's field of souls was ripe and ready for harvest, too. *Click!* The phone went dead in my hand. She had hung up on me! That was the last time I ever heard from my spiritual "vampire."

I tell this story to warn the Body of Christ that there are wolves in sheep's clothing out there wanting to bring destruction to the followers of Jesus. We must be awake, aware, and watching for the manipulative, draining behavior the devil can use to attack us.

5. Early Days of
Live Television

I just have to share some of the exciting dynamics of being involved in live Christian television produced from a secular studio. In the early days of Trinity Television, production occurred in the facilities of CKND, which is now known as the Global Television Network.

It's a New Day debuted on October 6, 1976, as a weekly program. At that time I was pregnant with our daughter, Becky. By the time I was expecting our son, Peter, two years later, the program was being seen five days a week. Warren and I were involved with singing on the program with Power in Praise. I was pretty much hidden in the group setting, but as time went on and it became more difficult to get everyone to take time from their jobs to be on the program, I began doing more solo work. By the time I was carrying my son, David, in 1980, I was pretty much singing on my own on the program.

I was sharing musically quite frequently on *It's a New Day*. As I mentioned, in those years we were using the CKND studios. During that time, we were back to back with another live program that aired right after *It's a New Day*. It was interesting to carry parts of the set away while the crew moved scenery, and the hosts of the CKND program came sweeping into the room. One of the hosts was a gentleman by the name of David Laurence. He later became a Christian and participated in Trinity Television's ministry. The CKND and Trinity Television people exchanged quick pleasantries as we vacated the studio and they set up for the CKND program. Through the late summer and early fall of 1980, my pregnancy was not too noticeable; by the end of my second trimester, I began to "blossom." The CKND people would see me frequently, as I would normally be on the set once or twice a month.

One day, David Laurence walked into the studio after *It's a New Day* ended, and the first words out of his mouth were, "Boy, have you ever gotten big!" Well, thanks David, I love you too! He was kidding around with me, of course, but I really did retain a lot of fluid with that third child. He was certainly well insulated!

Another day, for some unknown reason, the floor director decided that instead of standing and singing, it would be a good idea if I sat on a stool on the music set. I was willing to haul my pregnant girth onto a rickety CKND stool; I wanted to be accommodating! While Willard and Betty were doing their opening, I was behind the camera waiting to go on set to sing. I quietly tiptoed over to the music set, picked up my microphone, slid myself onto the stool, and put my foot onto the lower rung to steady myself and slide a little more onto the stool. *Crack!* The wooden rung snapped in two! I managed to keep my balance, my seat, and my dignity intact, but everyone stopped and stared for what seemed like an eternity. In reality, it was only a fraction of a second, but in "TV-time", minutes can seem like hours and a split second can seem like....well, you get the idea! My third child, David, came into the world on January 4, 1981. I was relieved in more ways than one! I continued to minister in music in various places, but my favorite place of ministry was always *It's a New Day*.

I had such a good time as I prepared music to sing so that the Lord would be lifted up and people's lives would be changed forever. I did not want people to just have a few minutes of "entertainment." My heart's desire was to touch people in their heart of hearts and affect them for eternity.

The hour drive into *It's a New Day* from Newton was always a joyful time of praising the Lord and anticipating what He was going to do through me as I surrendered this DNA house of clay! Those times were so precious with just Jesus and me; I would be crying tears of joy and adoration, and of course the makeup would be nearly cried off my face! I didn't care; I just wanted to be a vessel, a conduit, for the Lord to move through and out to the people watching.

I used to get phone calls from people who had been touched by the day's musical selection. One day a lady phoned to talk to me. She seemed almost apologetic as she explained why she had to call and talk to me. She explained that she had been watching *It's a New Day* for a short time, and she really wanted to know if the people who were on the program were sincere and real.

She was listening to me sing on this particular day and was impressed by the "polished performance", but she was not sure if it was just a "put on show" or if I was "for real." She said, "I hope this doesn't scare you, but I got in front of my TV set and looked right in your eyes to see if you were real, and you were! You really were singing from your heart, and I just wanted to tell you to keep up the good job of letting the Lord shine through you!" I thanked her and I had to admit to myself that part of me was a little "freaked out", but part of me was pleased that I had let my light shine so that people could see Jesus. Being on television for the Lord was certainly not for the faint hearted or the timid! For example, you certainly had to be brave to take a small child into the studio!

During the mid- 1980's, my two older children, Becky and Peter, were in school while David was still at home with me. On occasions when my babysitter would be unavailable, I would take David with me to the studio. He was pretty good at sitting quietly while the program went on, and he was really good for the three or four minutes that I was on set singing a song.

On one particular day in 1985, I had a really bad cold, so I "cheated" and brought a recording of our album, *He Loves You*, and lip-synched my solo, "Mountaintops." As I started the chorus, *"With your hand in my hand...."*, David ran onto the set and hid behind my skirt. I grabbed his hand and pulled him out beside me and continued to "sing" the song. The poor floor director had almost fallen over in his attempt to stop him, but David slipped past him. I chalked it up to another experience in live television!

A few days later, Power in Praise was doing a concert in a church. Afterwards, we were visiting with people in the fellowship hall. A lady came up to me and remarked that I looked so familiar to her, and then it dawned on her who I was. She said, "You're the mother whose little boy ran onto the set on *It's a New Day* a few days ago!" Yes, that was me and my Davy. By the way, David worked at Trinity Television from September 2000 to July 2006. It just seemed to be one of those things that was meant to be!

There were times when being in a secular television studio exposed you to sides of celebrities that, in the back of your mind, you knew existed, but you never dreamed in a million years were actually true! *It's a New Day* had just completed its broadcast, and the studio was transitioning from our show to the secular talk show produced by CKND. As we were vacating the studio, a well-known Hollywood actor/comedian was coming in to be the guest on the secular program.

He came into the studio holding the hand of another man. The famous comedian sort of swept in with this strange little man in tow as if it were a perfectly normal occurrence. I had David with me that day, and as those two fellows swooped in, I scooped David up into my arms and made a hasty exit. I wanted to be anywhere but there! You may ask if I hated those men, but of course I didn't! God loves us so much that He sent His son to be the way back into His house. I am saddened by the cheap imitation of love that Satan sells to people. It really made me thankful for the facilities that eventually housed Trinity Television, but it made me sad to know there are deceived people in the world who don't know the clean and pure love of the Lord. I was quick to take my child out of the atmosphere of poison that the enemy had spread. People are deceived when they say good is evil and evil is good. If I'm not mistaken, the judge of the universe has already pronounced what is within His law and what is against His law. Celebrity and money can never be a substitute for being one of God's kids and walking in His paths of righteousness. That gentleman is still alive today, and I think about him once in a while and pray for him to find the best and cleanest relationship, the only one that really works, the one that connects man to his Creator through our Lord Jesus Christ.

One guest on *It's a New Day* was Lee Nystrom, whose ministry touched men who had contracted HIV/Aids. This sweet, gentle man was used by the Lord to go into HIV hospices to tell these wounded souls about God's love for them. He would go and pray for them and expect God's healing hand to touch them. So many times God would perform a miracle as they would receive healing from the devastating effects of the disease, but the greatest healings would take place as these dying souls would make peace with the Creator. Lee was very forthright with the truth and would tell the men that if they received God's gift of healing they had to truly repent, turn from their wicked ways, and sin no more. In other words, they had to leave the lifestyle that had made them sick unto death. If they chose to ignore the extended hand of God's mercy and grace, they would lose their healing and die. Some took Lee's advice and kept their healing, while others did not take Lee's advice and lost their healing and died. Even as I write these words, I grieve for those who chose death instead of life, even after they were exposed to the great love of God.

It would be like a person who contracted lung cancer or liver disease as a consequence of their smoking and alcoholism being offered healing with the proviso that in order to retain their healing they had to abstain from tobacco and alcohol use. Seems a simple choice to make in order to enjoy a healthy body and lifestyle—abstain or suffer the consequences by lapsing into the very activity that caused the problem in the first place. On the last appearance that Lee Nystrom made on *It's a New Day*, I was privileged to be the musical guest for that day. Shortly after his appearance on the program, he went from this world into the world to come. Lee went to live in the Father's House.

Another powerful guest was Maury Blair, the survivor of terrible child abuse and the author of the book *Child of Woe*. We heard his testimony on *It's a New Day* and asked him to be the keynote speaker at a youth retreat that we were sponsoring. During the retreat we had a game of hide and seek. Maury won hands down because he had become an expert hider when he was trying to avoid the cruel beatings of his step-father. To let you know how "time marches on," Maury now speaks at senior's retreats. We can all identify with the process of aging—it's inevitable. It's my true and deep desire to be used until the last day, whenever that will be, for God's Kingdom as His ambassador.

One of the early guests on *It's a New Day* was Winkey Pratney. My husband really liked Winkey's admonition to "Rambo the old man," which meant to die to the old self every day and let God be on the throne of your life.

I have to mention one more guest who made an impression on me. Back in the Portage la Prairie YFC days, we had wonderful musicians come and minister before they became famous, such as Sandy Patty and another young woman who just radiated with Jesus' love, Pam Thum.

Pam's favorite line was, "In Jesus, you are Thumbody." It was a cute play on her name. At the YFC banquet when we were introduced to Pam, I saw a genuine worshipper in spirit and in truth. Her face would just shine with adoration for the King as she would lift her voice in praise. Pam became a favorite on *New Day*, and later her husband, Steve Marshall, would take part in telethons and regular broadcasts. One day during a telethon week, Pam was singing and I was at home watching and joining in the praise and worship that was pouring though the music. God was looking down on the two of us (Pam in the studio and me in my family room), and He impressed on my heart that as far as He was concerned we were in the same room and worshipping Him in the same spirit of unity. I was humbled and awed by that revelation. I decided to call in with my pledge for the coming year. Since the revelation was so fresh in my heart and mind, I began to share it with the phone counselor who had answered to take my pledge. As I bubbled over with enthusiasm about this insight, the counselor said, "Just a minute..." and handed the phone to Pam for me to share what God had just shown me. It was good to encourage her as much as it had encouraged me.

6. Healing Power
of Prayer—Part One

Through the years our lives have intertwined with Willard and Betty and their family. We can truly call them our dear friends, and we hold them as precious people that God has brought into our lives. They have been involved in some of our major family events, and they have been there when we have had our family crises. One serious crisis that we walked through involved our middle child, Peter.

We had been living and working in Newton since we began our building component manufacturing company in January of 1979. We actually moved to Newton in June of 1979 when our daughter, Rebecca, was two and half years old and our son, Peter, was six months old. Two years later, when Peter was two and a half years old and our David was six months old, we had one of those family crises that you move into and through only by the strength and peace of the Lord.

We had been at a neighborhood gathering. The children were all running around and having a good time. Peter was enjoying the playtime with the other children. Toward the end of the evening, he came and nestled close to me. I thought he was just tired out from the fresh air and playing with the other kids. We gathered our little family and walked home.

After we got home, Peter became feverish and began throwing up. I stayed up with him during the night, because every half hour he would be sick. After a while, he had nothing left in his stomach nor could he keep any fluid down. His color was not right, and even when he was lying down and sleeping his eyes were not closed. I did not know what the problem was, but I instinctively knew that there was something seriously wrong.

In the morning I called the doctor's office. They said to keep an eye on Peter during the day and try to get his fever down. If he didn't show signs of improving later in the day, I was to bring him into the office. I had been putting cold cloths on his head and trying to get him to keep down some children's aspirin, but he would throw up as soon as I gave him anything.

Something, or rather someone, kicked me into action mode in the middle of the day. I piled all of the kids into the car and sped to the doctor's office. They let me in right away, and the pediatrician on staff took one look at Peter and knew that this was a very sick little boy. I had been holding Peter on my lap, but the doctor said to put him down so he could walk. I was horrified as I put Peter down. His legs were stiff and he was almost falling over! The doctor, John Peters, said, "Take him right over to the hospital; I am going to order a lumbar puncture." I knew that the term "lumbar puncture" meant that this situation was extremely serious, serious enough for a spinal tap. I put the children in the car and drove across the street to the hospital. I didn't know what else to do, so I left four and half year old Becky and six month old David in their car seats with the windows cracked open and the doors locked. I carried Peter into the hospital, and the medical team told me to take him to the X-ray department right away. In the X-ray department, the technician placed Peter in the supports to take the necessary pictures. He commented that he knew this was a very sick child because he was falling asleep. I then took him to another room where the doctor performed the lumbar puncture, and Peter fell asleep as the procedure was being done!

As I was watching from the doorway, I had a sense that this was a desperately serious situation, yet I had a strange calm and peace that seemed to surround me and fill me. I literally felt like I was being carried. I knew I had to go and check on my other children, so I left the hospital to go to the parking lot. As I walked out of the door, I heard my car horn beeping loudly. Becky had escaped from her car seat and was having a great time playing with the steering wheel and blasting the horn, while David was fast asleep in his car seat. I looked across the parking lot and saw one of the ladies from our church standing by her car and looking around. I waved at her and she came over to my car. She told me that she had been visiting a lady from our Bible study who was in the hospital. She had just been getting into her car to go home when she heard the car horn blaring. She did not know where the sound was coming from, but she had been standing there for about five minutes trying to determine who was beeping the horn. I was so grateful that God had prepared this lady to be there at that time. She took Becky and David home with her, and I went back into the hospital. The doctor came over to talk to me and told me that the fluid he had taken from Peter's spine came out cloudy. The doctor said that without even testing the fluid he knew that Peter had a severe case of spinal meningitis. I knew this was not just serious, but life threatening! In fact, the doctor said that if I had waited much longer before bringing Peter into the hospital he would not have survived. As it was, the level of infection was very high, and he hoped that the antibiotics he had ordered would keep the damage from being too extensive.

Warren and I called the prayer line at Trinity Television. That wonderful resource of agreement in prayer was available to us to agree with those of like precious faith in the Lord. He will work in and through the amazing abilities of the medical personnel and the medicine that came from His plant kingdom, but after all is said and done it is the Lord who gave the gifts of healing and medicine in the first place. Medical people can only do so much, and then it is up to the sovereign king of the Universe to take charge and perform the healing. Willard and Betty called and said that they just "happened" to be coming out to Portage la Prairie for supper with some friends, and they would be happy to stop by the hospital to pray for Peter. Dr. Peters was so wonderful; he was truly prepared by the Lord in his quick diagnosis and action in getting the course of treatment started right away. He stayed in the hospital well into the evening.

Early in the evening, Willard and Betty came to pray over Peter. As they entered the hospital and rounded the corner to Peter's room, Dr. Peters and Betty saw each other and recognized one another from school! They both exclaimed, "Hello, what are you doing here?" Willard and Betty explained that they were here to see a little boy with meningitis, and Dr. Peters said, "He's my patient!" As Willard and Betty stood over Peter's bed and prayed for his healing, Dr. John stood in the doorway. When they finished praying, the doctor walked over to Peter's bed, put his hand on little Peter and, looking into his face, said, "You know that Jesus is going to heal you, don't you?" Peter nodded silently. The good news is that Peter was healed; he was released from the hospital within a week and he suffered no ill effects or impairment! The miracle is that Dr. Peters said it was the worst case of meningitis infection he had ever seen in his medical career, and he knew that God had brought all the events together for the healing of this child.

I have to insert some personal notes in regards to this wonderful, dedicated healer, Dr. John Peters. He was one of those tender hearted individuals who took his calling into medicine as a gift from the Lord to do good in the world through medicine. My understanding from people who knew him better than I, is that he had worked in the Health Sciences Center in Winnipeg. As a pediatrician in that facility, he saw many children who were victims of abuse and mistreatment. This caused his soul to agonize over the inhumanity and cruelty that can be perpetrated against innocent and vulnerable children. He had come out to Portage La Prairie to practice his medical arts in a smaller center where there wouldn't be the crushing volume of needless, manmade suffering. Unfortunately, no matter where you go on this planet, whether in large urban centers or small rural communities, man's heart is still wicked and in need of the transforming power of the work of redemption provided by Jesus' finished work on Calvary. The caseload of abuse in Portage was not to the same high volume that was to be found in Winnipeg, but the cases that he dealt with were still to the degree that they broke his heart.

One winter's day, Dr. John Peters went for a long walk and fell asleep in a snow bank and was set free from the pain of this world's sin and sadness. I never fully thanked Dr. John for his part in Peter's healing and recovery, but I am sure that our dear Lord Jesus will have a resounding, "Well done, good and faithful servant," for our brother on the day of the Lamb's Judgment Throne. Five years after his healing, when Peter was seven and half years old, I was notified that a series of tests had to be conducted as a follow up to determine the level of damage that occurred due to the severity of the infection. As the doctor in charge of the testing put Peter through the mental, physical, motor skill assessments, she kept looking at her chart and looking at Peter, then at me. At one point she looked at me and stated in a puzzled tone, "Mrs. Bracken, are you sure you have brought me the right child?" I asked her why she was asking and she answered, "Well, according to my chart and the infection level that is indicated, there should be some form of impairment either mentally or in motor skills or otherwise, but this boy's responses are all—perfect!" My response is to simply thank God for His miracle working power in operation through His obedient, faithful servants.

7. Adventures on Ministry Trips!

I would like to look back at some of the adventures that we have had with Willard and Betty on some of our trips with the ministry and during some of our touring experiences. One of the first trips we went on was a trip to Prince Albert for a telethon. I was impressed with how the Thiessens conserved the resources of the ministry. They would literally share a meal in a restaurant to cut down on the cost. They had an interesting way of saving gas called "avoid stopping and starting, even to change drivers!" We were on a stretch of double lane highway, I think between Saskatoon and Regina, and at one point the car we were in passed the Thiessen van, and Willard was driving. We went a little ahead of them and then slowed down a bit and they immediately passed us. The van was no longer being driven by Willard, and we knew they had not stopped! If memory serves me correctly, somehow Jeff was the new driver "miraculously" behind the wheel. Ah, the many talents those people have!

My husband served on the board of Trinity Television/ New Day Ministries from the mid 1980's until 2011, so we have had opportunity to help share the load that Willard and Betty, their family and staff had to carry. We have done our little bit, but it seems so small compared to the many areas of work carried out by these dear, selfless people. When you travel with such dedicated people and you see the many ways in which they conduct themselves in different settings, you gain an appreciation for the sacrifices that they make in order to get the job done. You could be sure that whether on the road or at home, faithful stewardship was exemplified by Willard and Betty to carefully and prayerfully administer each resource to its fullest extent with as little waste as possible!. In a world where there is so much greed and dishonesty, even in the ministries that are supposed to serve the Lord, it is wonderful to witness first-hand, up close and personal, people who are truly dedicated to being careful with God's money that is entrusted to them by the many faithful partners who have caught the vision of what a mighty and powerful tool television can be for the Kingdom of God.

8. Israel

We took one trip that is memorable because it was the trip of a lifetime—a trip to Israel, my dream of dreams! The wonderful part of that trip was that we were able to take our whole family. I am not even sure today, as I look back, how we were able to financially take that trip in 1992, except to say that it was one of those blessings from above. When Trinity Television advertised the package trip to the Holy Land and the Mediterranean cruise, we knew that it was the Lord's timing for us to go and see for ourselves the places of Bible history. We wanted our kids to enjoy the vacation and also experience the educational side of a trip of this magnitude. As Bob Meisner said to us one day, "There is just nothing like being there and seeing and hearing and tasting and smelling the actual experience of the Land of Israel." Our kids were in for an educational experience of a lifetime. We gave them control of the video camera and instructed them to record the trip. That was such a good idea; they got very creative with their video recording skills. They had to research the places we were scheduled to visit as well as inform, via the video record, what we had seen and done each day.

On the first leg of the trip, we flew from Winnipeg to New York City. From there, we flew to Paris for a re-fuelling stop.

The stop for fuel became an over-night layover as the plane required some repair before we could continue to Tel Aviv. It was an interesting delay because we were taken off the airplane while it was being fueled, then they let us back on board and kept us sitting and sitting. We knew something was not right when we were shown the movies and given our supper while we were still parked at the gate. After we had seen the movies and eaten our supper, our tour group started singing praise songs to the Lord—all forty of us in that planeload of people. I guess that the praise and worship music did something to the "powers that be," because they decided to deplane us and put us up in a hotel for the night. That unscheduled stopover could not dampen our mood. We lost a day in Israel, but we hit the ground running over the course of the next week and a bit. We saw Bethlehem and various parts of Jerusalem. We went to the Garden Tomb, which was empty, and celebrated communion. We prayed at the Western Wall and had an eye opening time as we observed the armed guards and the metal detector gates of that most holy of places. We felt for ourselves the atmospheric oppression and distress that hovers over the Temple Mount where the golden domed Al Aksa Mosque now sits as a monument to the god of Islam, Allah.

When we climbed to the place above the Western Wall, we were met by Arab guards at the top making sure the women were dressed in suitably non-revealing attire. Becky had on walking shorts, and even though she was only fifteen years old, this man approached her with an ugly, long, dark, hot skirt to wear. The atmosphere of fear and despair on the Temple Mount was upsetting her, and having this strange man give her this ugly garment to put on made her cry. Betty was very comforting to Becky and very sympathetic. She shared with us that when she first visited the Temple Mount, she had also encountered the oppressiveness of that place, and had to be practically carried along by others. Because of Becky's sensitivity to the realm of the spirit, she was reacting to the darkness of the enemy's spiritual stronghold of fear and domination. Becky needed a hug, so I gave her one. The same guard who had forced her to put on the skirt, came over and in broken English told us that no physical contact was allowed because of the "holiness" of that place. I was not afraid, but I was deeply saddened by the strong arm tactics of the Arab guards. I was amazed that they did not recognize that Becky was just a child needing comfort from her mother. I would have been more sympathetic to the need for "reverence" had there not been a group of Arab boys in shorts playing a rowdy game of soccer just a few steps away from where we were standing! It was truly an eye opening display of their double standard of ethics! The children of Ishmael need to know the God of Isaac, too.

When we left the Arab controlled section, the difference in the atmosphere was instantaneous—like night to day, darkness to light, oppression to freedom! When we were back in the Jewish Quarter, the feeling of relief was amazingly wonderful! For the most part, the kids had a great time. They were kept pretty busy with the video camera and the commentary and descriptions of where we went and what we saw. They gave themselves "stage names" and became an anchor news team. They even had commercials for bogus products like a plant food called "Fertilizer Green", and another one for a factory outlet for eye wear called "EyesRUs." I think they were a little ahead of their time; maybe Shopper's Optical saw some of our video "commercials."

We also went up to the mountain-top fortress ruins of Masada, where we saw a group of Israeli school children on a field trip. Children of that country must have armed body guards who escort them to the different sites. There were two parents accompanying them, each with a very visible automatic rifle.

Masada is the site on top of a flat mountain where a group of survivors from the siege of Jerusalem kept the Roman army at bay for a couple of years before the Romans gained access to the summit fortress, only to find that the survivors had committed suicide rather than be taken captive. It was a sobering reality check to view this monument to the tenacity and stamina of the Jewish people, who on Masada showed their fierce independence and aversion to tyranny.

The "Masada Model" of independence is no longer the mindset of the Israeli people. As shown by the school children's armed escort, the attitude of the Jewish people in this day and age is the "Samson Model." They will not go down without a fight, and, if necessary, they will not be afraid to take the enemy of Israel down, too! These people are determined to keep their homeland safe and secure. We had some thought provoking information given to us regarding who owns the land and why there is such a great tug of war going on over this tiny piece of real estate. When Mark Twain visited Palestine at the turn of the last century, he was disappointed to discover that the Holy Land was barren, neglected, and very under populated. He viewed Jerusalem and was amazed that there was so little to see. He only encountered a handful of Arabs in the region. There were large tracts of useless land, either desert or swamp. The few naturally fertile areas had tiny settlements of Arabs living a subsistent existence.

How did the land become transformed over the course of the next hundred years? We were given information as we toured, and I did my own research after I got home. In the nineteenth century a fund was established by the Jewish people to purchase tracts of land in Palestine from the Arabs. The Arab people gladly sold the malaria breeding swamps of Galilee and the arid desert in the Negev to the Jewish National Fund. The Jewish settlers who initially came to these areas had to endure terrible hardships to drain the swamps and irrigate the desert, but they persevered against the harsh elements and succeeded in reclaiming the land. The Jewish people came from many places, and due to the horrors of the Holocaust, they were highly motivated to go and live in their ancient homeland. The modern occupants of the land, the Arab people, have changed their minds about selling the worthless tracts of land now that the land is viable and productive. I am a little curious to know why the Jewish people are termed "occupiers" by the Arabs, as though they were living there illegally. It seems to me that the various conflicts that have occurred were usually started by Arab aggression, and the territory gained by the Israelis has been taken in accordance with the principle of the spoils of war going to the victor. I suppose the problem won't go away until the Prince of Peace returns to establish His Kingdom. Until that day, we can pray for the peace of Jerusalem, the Middle East, and its inhabitants—both Arab and Jew.

During our trip, we enjoyed the diversity of the many sites we toured. The group had a swim in the Dead Sea. Of course, one does not swim in the Dead Sea—one *floats* on the heavily mineralized water! Willard showed the technique to everyone by lying back in the water with his knees bent and holding his feet as he bobbed along as if in a reclining easy chair. We had an exciting trip to the Jordan River where a baptism service was held. Some of the people on the trip decided that it would be quite the experience to be baptized in the same river where Jesus was obedient to fulfill God's plan by having His cousin, John, administer his baptism. My heart was thrilled when our thirteen year old Peter decided it would be pretty neat to be baptized in the Jordan River.

Willard and Warren escorted Peter into the freezing cold water. There were nasty rocks in the river bed, and it was not a pleasant dunking like in a swimming pool or even a cozy tank in a church. Peter was really given the benefit of a first rate experience in truly going out of his comfort zone as a witness for the Lord in his life. I know that experience will stay with him throughout his life's journey!

The various places we visited in Israel had different significance attached to them for the people on the tour. There were some places, such as Capernaum, that taught us valuable lessons in the spirit as to the freedom that God has provided in Christ, as opposed to the bondage that religion brings. In this town situated on the North shore of the Sea of Galilee, we encountered two diverse sites that gave us a picture perfect example of the two kingdoms at odds in this world. The first site was the excavation of the ruins of a house dating back to the time of Christ. The archeological evidence is neither here nor there in identifying the occupants of this particular dwelling; however, the administrators of religious sites had determined that this had to be Peter the fisherman's residence. In looking at the outline of the remains of the home, one would not know the identity of the owner, but the site was treated as a significant find and given the name "Peter's House." The religious body in charge of this site had put a large iron fence around it, and anyone entering the area had to comply with the posted list of restrictions to visitors. For example, women had to be attired in modest clothing, and loud, boisterous behavior would not be tolerated. Upon entering the compound, one was met by a set of plans to build a shrine over the site, and an appeal for donations was posted. We looked at the area and respectfully complied with the posted rules, then we left and walked down the street.

At the end of the street was the site of the local synagogue. It was a building in ruins. The floor of the main room was intact. The walls were partially standing and there was no roof. You could go and stand in it without any barriers or posted signs. The site of the synagogue would be consistent with the place where the town's synagogue would be located. It was thrilling to think that you were standing in the exact same spot where Jesus had stood and taught! Willard and Betty did a home video of the place, with Willard giving the commentary on the location and the amazing truth that he was standing where Jesus stood! I was so blessed by the total contrast between the bondage and heaviness of religion and the freedom and joy we have in Jesus Christ. That lesson will stay with me for my life and into eternity.

As we were touring we were amazed at how green and vital everything was; our guide, Eli, explained that it had been an unusually wet winter. He kept saying things like, "Water is Life!" There were bright, wild flowers growing all over the hills. It was quite a spectacular sight! You almost forgot how much war that land has experienced since its rebirth in 1948. One time our bus stopped by the side of the road so we could look at the beautiful flowers, and Eli warned us not to venture too far off the road because of the danger of land mines. A couple of ladies seemed to be a little too far away from the safety of the roadside, and we had to call to them to please come back! It was one of those moments when you just click into careful "police/ Mommy mode." You just wanted to rush over and drag them back to the bus! All was well, but the realization of what was out there made me keep my kids a little closer to my side. There are many other things that I could share regarding our trip through the Holy Land, but I will have to save that for another time.

The first part of the trip was the tour through Israel. The second part of the tour was a cruise to various sites in the Mediterranean. After our busy time of touring in Israel, we were looking forward to the leisurely pace of the cruise. We boarded our ship, the Greek liner The *Atalante* (pronounced "At-a-lan-tay"), in the port city of Haifa. It was interesting to see how people reacted to ship life. Our cruise ship was an older model built in the 1950's. There were lots of stairs, no stabilizers, and the diesel engines belched out black smoke from the stacks. Warren and Willard had a great time playing ping pong under the sooty cloud that poured down on them from above!

The crew was Greek, and we had a lovely gentleman as our server in the dining room. We could not speak Greek, and he could not speak English, but we communicated through smiles and gestures and broken bits of language. We became friends by seeing each other every day, three times a day, at our meal seating. He was a grandfatherly type of person who took great care in making sure our kids were taken care of and given their food, some of it being a tad strange—like octopus/squid with its suckers plainly in view! We were given a small cruet of some clear liquid, and he poured out our portions into tiny glasses. The children will never forget their first and last taste of the Greek liquor Ouzo! Apparently this licorice flavored "fire water" is dispensed to everyone regardless of age. I guess it's considered Greek mother's milk. We were careful to monitor the various food and beverage items offered to us after our first supper aboard this quaint, slightly antiquated vessel. An experience of this type can certainly give you an appreciation for our Canadian foods and cultural amenities. Our waiter was a goodwill ambassador of sorts. As well as sharing some pictures of his children and grandchildren with our family, he seemed to take a shine to my children. I think they made him miss his family a little bit. Meeting people like this man, whose life is one of service, makes you appreciate the human family and gives you a glimpse into the reason why our Heavenly Father loves us so much. Even though we are not perfect, we each have our moments of showing our divine origin in our kindness and caring for one another.

The ship took us to different ports of call. We went to the Isle of Rhodes and viewed a crusader castle. We traveled to Turkey and toured the ruins of Ephesus. Ephesus deserves some extra focus as I share a few impressions of that impressive place. Our guide for the Ephesus tour was a young Turkish woman who was very knowledgeable about the times and history of the area. As we walked down the main thoroughfare, she pointed out the statues along the colonnade. Some of them were without heads. She explained that the statues were constructed in such a way that the heads were removable on purpose. The reason? It was too costly to make a whole new statue for the latest famous person, so they made a generic male or female body and changed the heads. I guess this is the antiquity equivalent of our society's fifteen minutes of fame. She pointed out a very interesting statue that was just off the side of the road. It was a conquering hero, possibly a Roman warrior, but the most amazing thing was that this statue (which had its head, just by the way) had one foot on a sphere, or globe. The tour guide told us that this was a depiction of a conqueror with his foot on the conquered world—planet Earth. Isn't it interesting that there are people today who still believe that the world is flat!

We were also shown the public toilet. This place was fascinating because of its arrangement. The toilet area was this huge space, around the perimeter of which were a series of holes in the stone seats. The guide said that the seats used to be overlaid with marble, and the rich people would send their slaves to sit and warm the spot before the rich person would go and "do their business." I suppose the slaves were under orders not to enjoy themselves! The other eye opening thing was the fact that the seats were arranged in a semi-circle around an empty space. The empty space, according to the guide, used to have various entertainers singing, dancing, juggling—just plain old entertaining the public potty patrons. I have a home video of Willard and Betty sitting side by side and Willard joking that when he was a boy they had "two-seaters," but never anything like this! I love to hear about Willard's boyhood on the farm in Alberta, but I think that was a little too much information for me!

One more Ephesus story is both funny and sort of sad because it shows that people's hearts are so very far removed from where they are supposed to be as bearers of the Father Creator's image. As we proceeded down the main street, the guide drew our attention to a flat stone on the side of the road. I thought it was just a large paving stone with decorations engraved on it. The guide told us that this was the main route for the sailors to take from the pier into town. This stone's engraving was the Ephesian equivalent of a billboard advertising the local brothel straight ahead at so many paces.

The local brothel was located across the street from the best preserved facade in the town—the library building. This beautifully detailed structure had a dark side to it, according to the guide's commentary. The Ephesian men would tell their wives that they were "going to the library." This was true. They were going to the library, and then they were taking the tunnel that ran under the street into the brothel. How sad and deceptive for these poor people. I was impressed with the preservation of the ruins of that place and the various stories attached to the structures and the lives of the people of Ephesus. I can read the Letter to the Ephesians from Paul with a little more understanding of what they had to deal with as a society.

We were given the option to go to Smyrna or take a bus tour of the town. We were a little tired of ruins and opted for the bus tour. We drove around and ended up in a little candy store where we bought genuine Turkish delight. This was exciting for our kids, who had been raised with the C. S. Lewis tales of Narnia. They had always wanted to try Turkish delight; however, the actual experience of tasting the candy was a little below their imagination's build- up of the Narnian confection. The children brought a few pounds of the real stuff home for their school classmates to sample.

Our adventures on the cruise were supposed to include the Isle of Patmos, but the sea was too rough for the tenders to take us over to the place of the Apostle John's exile. What we could see of the island gave us the impression of a barren rock. It was actually a really good place for John to commune with the Lord and receive the book of the Revelation—there is really nothing to look at on that place! The day when the sea was roughest was actually funny, because Warren spent a lot of his youth in Sea Cadets and later the Naval Reserve. He loved the sea, and the rougher the better. While people were huddled around the deck in their chairs, wearing their life preservers and looking very green, Warren was standing in the salt spray, laughing and ignoring the dirty looks he was getting from his fellow sea goers. The balance of our trip had us viewing the sites in Athens from the Parthenon on the Acropolis, to the site of the Mar's Hill address by Paul in the book of Acts. Our life changing trip was over, but we were filled with new insight and great memories.

A few days after we returned home, Peter was in school and the teacher had them open their social studies book to a certain page. Peter's eyes lit up as he looked at the picture of the Parthenon and he exclaimed, "Hey, I've been there!" The class was impressed. I think his teacher was a little envious, because he said with mock disdain, "Oh shut up, we know you've been there!" All in all, my children will never forget the trip that we took, the many things we saw and experienced, and the pure joy of coming home with a treasury of so many rich memories. I had to take the time to share this part of our adventures with

Trinity Television, because I don't know if we would ever have gone to Israel if Willard and Betty had not been led to host that tour. It had a great impact on our family spiritually, emotionally, and relationally. I would encourage anyone to go to Israel with a tour. The facilities are usually first class, and the buses that are used to transport tourists are clean and air conditioned. We had an eighty-four year old lady on our tour, so age is never a deterrent to travelling to the Holy Land. Warren and I took another Israel tour with the Thiessens years later and helped out making sure the people stayed together and that everyone made it onto the bus. I found these trips to the Holy Land to be informative, educational, and spiritually uplifting as we saw the sights, walked where Jesus walked, and saw for ourselves evidence of the Jewish homeland, God's Land.

The last Israel trip that we took with Willard and Betty had its own unique flavor. We were there when Yasser Arafat was holding court in Ramallah, and Andrew White was conducting shuttle diplomacy missions to bring peace to the region. Dr. White is now the head of the archdiocese of Baghdad. We met his travelling companion, Dr. Ravi Zacharias, and were impressed by both men's humble, Christ-like demeanor. That tour had another interesting facet. A Canadian woman from the University of Alberta was travelling alone and had asked the travel agency if she could join a tour. Our tour was the only one being run by Canadians, so she joined us. She was introduced to us crazy Canadian Christians, and we all had the pleasure of sharing our stories and testimonies with her. One evening when we were sitting in the hotel's lobby lounge after a day of touring, Dr. Zacharias and Dr. White came in from their day of diplomatic work. They talked with this young woman, who had many questions. Even though they were tired, they took the time to patiently answer her, and at the end of the evening gave her one of Ravi's books on Christian apologetics.

I felt humbled to be a witness to this quiet event. This young woman became more and more at peace through the course of the tour. When we were on the Mount of Beatitudes in the quiet gardens, she professed that she had been searching for the peace that we all seemed to have, and she wanted it for herself. Amazing grace! I have to say, "Thank you for your obedience, Willard and Betty. I know that hosting tours is a lot of work, and we appreciated the opportunity to share them with you."

The front and back cover of the Power In Praise album sponsored by Trinity Television titled "I'm Coming Home, Lord" and underneath is the insert page showing us 30 plus years after.

Betty, Me, and Warren—balloons in the background must mean a Telethon night!

Willard and Warren at another Telethon. One day Warren was chatting with Willard on the telephone and Warren said "You know Willard, of all the people I know–long pause–you're one of them!!" There was a moment of silence and then a loud burst of laughter as only Willard can deliver!

This picture was taken at a Trinity Television banquet evening.

Singing for my King Jesus on It's A New Day*–I was always amazed at how God would dovetail the message in the music with the guest's message.*

Another Telethon evening with Betty and Willard standing in front of the phones. Warren is just behind them taking a pledge.

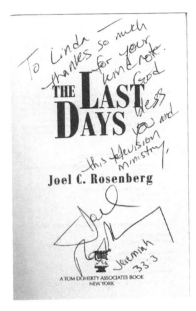

THE LAST DAYS

Joel C. Rosenberg

A TOM DOHERTY ASSOCIATES BOOK
NEW YORK

The title page from Joel Rosenberg's book that he signed for me. The note that he referred to is as follows:

Dear Mr. Rosenberg:
I am sending this note along with the copy of your book "The Last Days" to ask a favour. This book came to my attention as I was grocery shopping at the Publix in Lake Wales, Florida in July. I don't normally buy books at the grocery store, but I was compelled to pick up a copy of this book. I did not even read it until I got home to Canada. As I began by reading the acknowledgments, I was struck by the fact that you called your sons your "prayer warriors" and as I read the book, I knew I was reading a work that was written by someone who loved the Lord.

Through several "Divine Appointments" I realized that buying the book at Publix was the first link in a chain of events that would culminate in your being here and as the details are too numerous to be written in this short note, suffice it to say that I am Happy that you got to be here, today.

To make a very long story relatively short, I would appreciate it if you would sign this copy as a testament to the loving Father Who has guided His people. I would also like to take this opportunity to encourage you as you follow the Lord's direction for your life. Thank you for your kind attention and may God richly bless you.
Sincerely,
Linda G. Bracken

I had given the book and letter to my son, David, who worked for Trinity Television as a camera operator, studio manager, and editor.

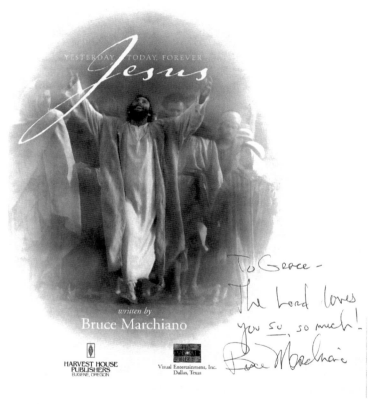

The inscription to my mother-in-law Grace from actor/author
Bruce Marchiano on the day she was able to sit in the studio and
listen to his interview. She was so excited when she said "I can
hardly wait to tell the girls that I met Jesus!"

May 25 1996–the Trinity Television choir at the Winnipeg Arena when we took part in the Celine Dion concert's final number "Call The Man."

My daughter Becky is in the front row second from the left looking very drawn and pale as she was going through the ordeal of her fiance Ryan battling Meningitis just one week before their wedding scheduled for June 1. I am in the second row just behind Celine's shoulder.

This is a page from the December 2001 New Day Report, the monthly newsletter. The staff Christmas photo includes our son David (front row left)

9. Healing Power of Prayer—Part Two

My children have all been exposed to the solid Biblical teachings from Trinity Television's many resources. *Follow Me*, the early children's series, was viewed by my kids, and later *Sonshiny Day* had a special place in their lives. Willard and Betty's daughter, Audrey Meisner, was the host and producer of the children's program. She called one day and asked if Becky was interested in helping with the production. Becky took the role of Squirt, the Super-Smart and Speedy Squirrel, with great delight. Later she was given the role of Cherry Buckleberry. She also helped out with other puppet duties and developed a growing appreciation for the amount of work that goes on behind the scenes of television production. She learned what the term "hurry up and wait means." That means that all of the puppets and personnel would be called to the set and be ready for their cue to begin the scene. There would be a big panic to get to your place, and then nothing would happen for the longest time. Either the cameras were not set up right, or the sound guy had a problem to fix, or the director (Audrey's husband and co-producer, Bob) had to do "something," and on it would go. So you sat and waited. It seems to me there is a passage in 2 Peter 1 about giving diligence and adding to your faith virtue, to virtue, knowledge, to knowledge self-control, to

self-control perseverance, to perseverance Godliness, to Godliness brotherly kindness and to brotherly kindness love. At the
end of it all you get to be fruitful, and of course one of the fruits
of the Spirit is patience! Yes, my Becky received some good lessons being part of *Sonshiny Day*. She is an amazing and Godly
woman today, thanks in part to the discipline and hard work
of being part of creating Jesus-based children's programming.

When Becky was preparing to be married, we had an adventure of another sort. To begin the story, Becky, Warren,
and I were invited to participate in a Gospel choir that was
to perform the song "Call The Man" during the finale of the
Winnipeg concert that was scheduled as part of Celine Dion's
Falling Into You tour. The concert date was Saturday May 25,
1996, one week before Becky's June 1st wedding day.

We had practiced the song for about a month with the
other participants, who were various musicians that Laurence, Trinity Television's music director, had invited to make
up the Gospel Choir. In the midst of pre-wedding activity, we
also had the choir practices. Becky and I were thoroughly enjoying the practice sessions. Becky's fiancé, Ryan, worked for
our truss manufacturing company. On Thursday morning,
the 23rd of May, Becky got a phone call from one of Ryan's
co-workers who had arrived at Ryan's house to take him to
work. Ryan was delirious, feverish and uncoordinated. Ryan's
friend called Becky to take him to the hospital. The diagnosis
came back as Meningitis! Earlier in the week, another friend
of Ryan's had been diagnosed and treated for the infectious
disease. This friend had been at Ryan's bachelor party, and everyone had received preventative treatment except Ryan.

We don't understand the oversight in not giving treatment to Ryan, but God had His plan all worked out. We believed that Ryan could be prayed for and healed as easily as
our son Peter had been, but we had to be sensitive to Ryan's

unbelieving family members who thought all we cared about was our wedding plans and not their son. We wrestled with what to do, all the while being involved in the preparation for the Celine Dion concert. On Saturday the 24th, Becky and I went to the arena to get ready for our part in the choir. Becky stated at one point that she did not want to be there; she would rather be at the hospital with Ryan. She later admitted that it was a relief of sorts to have a break. It was a good distraction to be learning the little swaying motions and side to side steps that would accompany the song. It certainly seemed appropriate to be singing "Call The Man," which is a song about looking for God to come and be part of our daily lives. Way to go, Celine! Good song choice! It certainly bolstered our faith.

Willard and Warren went to the hospital to pray for Ryan. Becky and Ryan had to make the hard decision about the wedding, since Ryan's condition did not seem to be progressing fast enough toward healing. I had called Trinity Television's prayer line and agreed in prayer with the counselor, and by faith we really felt that Ryan would be healed and all ready for June 1st. I am glad to say that Ryan and Becky did get married on June 22nd, 1996, and Warren and Willard officiated on that day of great rejoicing. Today, our son-in-law is the co-manager in our Florida truss plant. He's one sharp guy!

10. Fast Forward— The Christian Media Centre

I can remember when Trinity Television's offices took up residence on St. Anne's road and created a studio to produce extra programming. Each step seemed bolder and more innovative than the previous steps. As Willard and Betty's faith increased, God increased their vision and their capacity to believe for greater impact in the marketplace for the kingdom of light. Their faith did not crumble, even on the day that CKND told Trinity Television that there would be no more live programming after a certain date. That event put them into search mode, looking for a building to accommodate their needs and the criteria needed to send the live feed to CKND's facilities. That whole journey of faith is chronicled in Audrey Meisner's book, *On The Brink Of Explosion*. Willard conscripted board members to help find a suitable facility with the proper line of sight to CKND's tower. They searched and found an old aluminum extrusion plant on 1111 Chevier Blvd., just off Pembina Highway. Warren's civil engineering background was pressed into service to help revamp the building's cavernous interior into useable zones for banquet halls, meeting rooms, a commercial kitchen, lobby, board room, chapel, offices, production suites, and studio space. One of the wide open spaces was divided vertically, and by utilizing floor trusses, an upper mezzanine floor was created. A skylight system was developed over the atrium to bring in natural light.

My take on the new building at 1111 Chevrier, was from the perspective of trying to find the studio in the midst of the demolition and reconstruction of the factory-turned-television facility. It was truly adventurous making my way from the offices waayyy in the front of the building to the studio waayyy in the back. When they were taking out the concrete floor to refurbish the plumbing, you had to be part- mountain- goat- part- tightrope -walker! Okay, so I'm exaggerating just a little bit, but not much! The best word that I can use to describe the work in progress was "cavernous." It was dark, treacherous, and it echoed like a cave. I had to say, though, that reaching the studio was a wonderful experience in fulfillment. One of the first finished spaces was the new studio, which was large and inviting and warm—mainly because the Spirit of the Lord was at home there and there was no competition with the residual atmosphere of the enemy. Worship could flow freely and sweetly in that place. I must also say that part of me missed the witness that we had in the other studios. I know that our presence was a powerful testimony to those dear folks at CKND.

The Christian Media Center at 1111 Chevrier eventually was completed, and everyone who walked through the facility was impressed with the beauty of the building and the beautiful atmosphere of peace that was there. I know that the many banquets and events hosted by the facility have been "Five Star" class affairs, which was a far cry from our first fundraising pancake breakfasts in the large, unfinished factory. You had to really use your imagination back in those days to "see" what the finished product would look like, and even then it was a huge stretch! I think it's interesting to note that Betty did a lot of baking and food prep for some of the conferences and other events. She is such a talented and giving person who has a servant's heart and a true gift of hospitality. After an event, you would see Jeff Thiessen, Willard, or Bob Meisner manning the vacuum cleaner or putting tables away. If you were there to see that, then you were probably pitching in and helping tidy up the room, too!

When you walked in through the front door you were met by the friendly receptionist sitting in a beautiful oak work station in the middle of the lobby. On the wall to the right was the spectacular "Tree of Remembrance." It had brass leaves engraved with different scriptures and the names of people who contributed to the building project. It was a beautiful reminder of the many faithful ones who had stood with Trinity Television through the years in financial and prayerful support. Speaking of prayer, also on the right was the hallway leading to the prayer counselors' offices. The many volunteer counselors took special courses and had at the core of their hearts the deep desire to see the hurting ones who called in healed and set free. It was a true labor of love.

A doorway into the book store was a doorway into a rich resource of materials representative of the many ministries that had shared on *It's a New Day*. I can say from personal experience that the many and varied titles seemed too many to choose from, yet I wanted to read them all! Video and audio tapes, books, books, and more books could be found here, as well as music tapes. One could spend a day or two just browsing through this tiny room filled with life giving material. The various offices were found through a doorway to the left, but the view that beckoned to you through the middle double doors was that which led you into the light-filled atrium. From this central point, you could look back at the board room along the south wall. Opposite was the etched glass wall enclosing the prayer room. The glass depicted God singing and speaking into being all of creation. On the same wall were the doors leading into the conference room. This large area has seen many banquets and conferences. It was a warm and inviting banquet hall, which had been rented by private individuals for wedding receptions. The large professional kitchen was accessed from both the conference room and the hallway that led to the studios. Another access way, from the atrium, led to the CHVN radio studio and offices on the south side of the media center.

Another wall in the atrium showed plaques of dedication for those who had contributed further into the ministry of Christian television via Trinity. As you moved through the atrium, you could see pictures on the walls. There were photos of different staff members and some of the well-known people who had been participants on telethons and in various conferences and programs. Down the hallway, leading to the studios and production area, were more pictures of some of the notable guests. During a buffet banquet years ago, we were making our way down the hall in the lineup to get our supper when I noticed that the pictures did not have any plaques telling who was who. We knew people like Willard and Betty and others like Mayor Bill Norrie and Pat Boone and Dale Evans, but I guess I just felt the need to identify some of the more unknown people in the photographs. I was thrilled to be given the inspiration to do this project; it has enhanced the enjoyment of walking down memory lane as one views the photographs of these many special people.

The hallway had access to the staff lounge and the kitchen. There was also a side hall leading to the guest suite. This area was very special because it allowed Trinity to host some of their guests on site. It made it very convenient for the guests, as they had all the comforts of a suite hotel without the expense. They could relax and read or watch television. There was a refrigerator that was stocked with some complimentary snacks and soft drinks. In the past, Willard and Betty had hosted guests in their home. This had made for some enduring friendships; however, it could be a little tiring to have house guests as well as work full time. I am sure that as much as Willard and Betty have the gift of hospitality, they were relieved when the guest suite was being used. The staff who looked after the guest suite told me once that they had had two outstanding guests who left the suite in pristine condition—Ken Gaub and Bruce Marchiano. I just had to share that because both of these men have more said about them later on in this story, and I wanted to let you know that they are exceptional and outstanding people of integrity and honor who think about others before themselves. Hold that thought until later!

Further down the main hallway was the green room, where guests prepared for the program by chatting with Willard. The production suite and production offices were located at that side of the building, as were studios "A" and "B". There was an access hallway back to the conference room. It had certainly been amazing to watch this drab, empty factory become a hub of production and creative activity for the Kingdom of God. To think that everyone who supported Trinity Television had a part in that miraculous place is truly exciting!

Secular media rented the facilities at Trinity and were impressed with the size and quality of the Christian Media Center. Studio "A" was so large that it was used by CBC to house the set for the children's television program *Fred Penner's Place*. The set for this program was quite impressive. It was like walking into a forest—very disneyesque! Part of this massive set is visible through the windows of Mr. and Mrs. Buckleberry's kitchen in the *Sonshiny Day* children's series written by and featuring Audrey Meisner. Speaking of the "Buckleberry" characters, one day Audrey was looking for some creative input for new characters and out of my fertile imagination popped Cherry Buckleberry! Audrey loved the name and made one of the red headed puppets "Cherry," and one of the red headed male puppets Cherry's twin brother, "Chuck." One more piece of intriguing *Sonshiny Day* trivia is that the set for Sonshiny Mountain was used by the production company filming a T.V. movie about the Osmonds. The production company was all over the Christian Media Center—in the board room and green room, as well as the studio. It was fun to watch our beautiful facility being seen on an American network. The Sonshiny Mountain prop was used in a scene that was supposed to be from the early *Donny and Marie* variety shows. This is rather special considering that we were being compared to professional and commercially funded production houses. What a testimony of honor given to our King when a ministry lifts up the Lord and maintains integrity and humility.

11. In Christ We Live and Move and Have Our Being

Being in the Christian Media Center gave a person the feeling of "rightness" in the atmosphere of this God-ordained facility. I attended various functions and conferences in this beautiful building, and I always came away with a sense of being a witness to God's perfect plan perfectly being worked out through the ministry housed there. You just knew that there were life changing and life enhancing opportunities being fulfilled through Trinity Television on a lot of different levels, apart from the obvious ministry on Television. For myself, I had been challenged, fed, uplifted, exhorted, and prompted to stretch outside of my comfort zone by being involved in some of the extra meetings that had been offered by Trinity Television. Some of the extracurricular events that stand out in my mind had to do with some of the superb guests of world class quality and caliber who have been at the Christian Media Center for special meetings. Because I have been privileged to participate in some of these events, and have had my life impacted by the teachings of the guests, I would like to mention some of the wonderful people who came to the Christian Media Center.

Tamara Winslow is a lady of many talents and abilities. She is a prophetic singer and songwriter and pianist with a powerful teaching and speaking ministry. She conducted a number conferences based on a variety of themes, which were well attended and quite successful in building up the Body of Christ. Because my husband was a board member of Trinity Television, we were privileged to be part of special teaching and prayer times with Tamara, as the Board met with her to seek the Lord on behalf of the ministry and to build the individual board members' faith. Tamara has taught on the Holy Spirit. We were given deep insight into the member of the Godhead who is so often misunderstood and misrepresented by the Church. His position and working through the Old Testament into the New Testament and on into the future, as well as His personality, were given a thorough and respectful treatment. Thank you, Tamara, and well done!

I attended a very special luncheon for Women In Ministry. The guest speaker for the occasion was Lois Burkett. The teaching and challenge of the day was to identify ourselves correctly. Sometimes it is too convenient to say "I'm Warren's wife," or "my children's Mother," or that my identity is found in my occupation. Instead, we should say that our identity is found in who we are in Christ Jesus—children of the living God! Another poignant facet to that meeting was the special music presented by Lois Burkett's friend, Lucretia Shaw. Lucretia was beautiful, inside and out. Her sweet spirit and amazing voice brought us closer to the throne room of the Father. She walked through the room full of ladies singing "His Eye Is On The Sparrow" a cappella. A short time after this event, Lucretia and her husband were involved in a private plane crash. Lucretia did not survive the plane crash, but I know she is safe with our Heavenly Father.

On another occasion, Trinity Television sponsored a "Financial Freedom" Seminar. I was blown away by the practical and dynamic principles of financial management that were presented by the different teachers. It was a RICH experience, to say the least. There have been many teachers who have given us wisdom on finances. Paul Johnson is the author of the *Canadian Financial Handbook for Christian Living*. He also wrote a book titled *Stairway to Financial Freedom*. Just those titles alone will tell you how much value there was in this gentleman's teaching. We had advice from Craig Hill, who has been on *It's a New Day* frequently. We learned that "mammon" is not another word for "money." Mammon is a demon, a spirit, a principality. During Jesus' time, the false god, Mammon, was the recipient of prayers by deceived people hoping for prosperity and finances. Money is not our source. God is our source, but more than that—God is our goal. We don't follow God for what He can give us. We follow God because He is worth following, no matter where He leads. The deceiver substitutes money as our goal instead of God, who is the true supplier of our needs. All of our resources, every good and perfect gift, comes from God the Father in Heaven. Craig certainly challenged some of our old thinking patterns!

Craig impacted our lives again when he spoke at a family camp where Power in Praise was ministering. At that family camp we also met and were encouraged by Bob and Barbara Jenkins, who were stalwart friends and supporters of *It's a New Day*. They had been guests on the program from the earliest days. One more special person who gave generously to us was Mr. Ken Gaub. Ken is a very unusual speaker in that he is more like a stand-up comedian! His book, *God's Got Your Number!*, is about the variety of ways that God gets through to us using the most miraculous, supernatural, over the top, out of this world, mind boggling tactics! He certainly knows where we are, who we are, and how to get in touch with us, even when we are not expecting Him to call us! Ken was the last speaker of the day at the seminar. We were working on information overload, but

Ken brought us information and refreshment in a warm, humorous package. Besides being a gifted speaker, Ken gives the best neck and shoulder massages! The one day seminar was jam packed with speakers and sessions, and Ken had us stand in a row and rub the person's neck in front of us. Ken was a featured Trinity Television guest for many years and will always remain one of my favorites. I have more "Ken" stories later.

"Delight of Discovery," the National Women's Conference held October 2 to 4th, 1998, featured Bunny Wilson. My daughter, Becky Blair, attended this weekend with me, and we were privileged to share a musical selection in the final session. It was a very special mother/daughter bonding time.

I attended several conferences specifically targeting business leaders. The first took place shortly after the "Financial Freedom" conference. Trinity Television invited Dennis and Megan Doyle, founding members of Nehemiah Partners, a ministry designed to network and mentor Christian business leaders to assist in the call to restore biblical values to the marketplace. The daylong seminar also included their pastor, Rich Marshall. We learned about incorporating God's Principles into our business principles. Rich taught us about "King's" (business leaders), "Priests" (ministry leaders) and the blended "Kingly Priests" or "Priestly Kings," which is what my licensed-minister-of-the-Gospel/businessman husband would be, if you can follow what I mean!

Another one day conference, led by Dr. J. Victor and Catherine Eagan, took me into a personal realm of faith as they shared on "Workplace Wisdom." Dr. Eagan is a successful orthodontist, and his beautiful wife, Catherine, worked in the world of high finance through investment banking for a couple of decades before being called to join her husband in business. The workbook was valuable for self-assessment and evaluation in the areas of personal relationships and work ethics.

The Lord seemed to use their "Workplace Wisdom" to light a fire under me regarding taking authority over the atmosphere in, around, and over our business.

Warren and I had dedicated our company to the Lord from the start of our business, but we had been sort of passive about daily bringing situations and people to the Lord's Throne. I decided to do a "prayer walk" through our plant on a Saturday, anointing the work stations with oil and praying over the operators and various staff and personnel. Then I became excited about the possibility of setting up a prayer room right in our building. The perfect room presented itself in the form of a vacant office a few steps above our accounting/payroll office. I had been praying for our employees for several years, using the timecards as points of contact, and the thought of having a room where I could go and intercede for different situations and people was too exciting for words!

The fruit of our obedience will certainly be revealed in Heaven, but it is good to get feedback here and now! Our prayer journal contained many entries and many answers to prayer. People's hearts were becoming soft to the Gospel, and we saw a deeper hunger and thirst for the Word in our Christian workers. It was so good to be able to contact the *It's a New Day* prayer line and agree with the prayer counselors. The joy of having the resource of agreeing in prayer with those of like precious faith was beyond description! Since I was challenged to start a prayer room and intercessory prayer journal on behalf of our employees after attending the conference with Victor and Catherine Eagan, my eyes had been opened to the opportunity to minister and witness to our employees and fellow co-workers in our work place.

One day our truss plant production manager, who is a dear brother in the Lord, came to me and asked if I had been praying for a certain employee in any special way. It so happened that

I had been asking God to touch this person's heart after they had a death in the family. This employee had started watching Christian television, and actually approached our production manager with questions on how to make God a part of your life. That was pretty much a confirmation that we were on the right track!

Because of Willard and Betty's vision to get business people to really see themselves as missionaries in the workplace, my husband and I have been challenged to go the extra mile on behalf of our company. It has confirmed to my husband and I that we are in "full time ministry" by the very nature of our love for the Lord and our desire to carry His truth and integrity into our lives every day. I would like to relay a brief account of what we have experienced in our industry as we have let our light shine and our colleagues in the truss industry have watched our lives and evaluated the fruit of our testimony.

Many years ago we were attending a truss industry conference in Orlando at Disney World. The conference was being held at the Contemporary Resort attached to the Magic Kingdom Theme Park. During that conference, a couple in our industry decided to get married. They asked Warren to "officiate" as the minister, and the lady's sister, who is a Justice of the Peace, would perform the legal part of the ceremony. The special music team was comprised of myself and two of our employees who were also attending the business conference. The people in our industry know that we are Christians, and they have a respect for our values because we do not come across as "religious" or "condemning" or "no fun."

The Trinity Television business seminars had confirmed to us that God cares about our business and our witness in the business community. Christians should have the highest level of integrity, honesty, and quality in their products and relationships with employees, suppliers, and customers. The witness we have to those watching us speaks loudest by our actions first and then by our attitudes and words. We are called to *"let your light shine before others, so that they may see your good works and give glory to your Father who is in heaven."* (Matthew 5:16)

Finances, business, healing, the Holy Spirit, encouragement to women in ministry, and walking by grace are just a few of the topics covered by special gatherings that Trinity Television has sponsored! All that and the daily encouragement of people who love Jesus being seen over the television airwaves.....wow!

12. Name-Dropping 101

As I have reminisced about different events, I have mentioned some people who have been influential and instrumental in my journey of faith and life, specifically with Trinity Television. Some of the people who have been guests have made an impact on me, as I have been able to see some "celebrity" type people "up close and personal."

I remember Betty mentioning the first "celebrity" she had ever encountered, the wife of the late Roy Rogers, Dale Evans. Dale was in Winnipeg to participate in the *It's a New Day* telethon. She was also scheduled to be the guest on the daily television program. Betty recalls being very nervous about meeting this high profile Hollywood actress and American icon whose title was "The Queen of the West." Dale came into Winnipeg on the morning of the program and was ushered into the CKND studios. She asked Betty to show her to the lady's room. Betty took her to the washroom and found that all her nervousness melted away as Dale chatted easily with Betty as if they were old friends. I think Betty really felt comfortable when Dale kept up the conversation, even when she was in the stall "doing her thing"! The bottom line is, celebrity or not, we are all pretty much the same. Dale has since joined her husband in eternity, and they are both enjoying the happy trails of Heaven.

My first up close and personal encounter with a celebrity took place when Donna Douglas came to Winnipeg to be part of the telethon, and the Thiessens had a reception in their home for board members and some supporters of the ministry. Donna is a lovely lady who gained her fame portraying Elly Mae Clampett in the Sixties television show *The Beverly Hillbillies*. She had become a Christian, gone to a Bible College, and was using her celebrity status to share God's love with people. The reception was typically centered on Betty's wonderful and delicious cooking, and we all admired the many culinary surprises laid out buffet style on the dining room table. We took our plates and got in line. I was following a dear lady, Edith Wimbush, who, along with her husband Jim, had been friends of Willard and Betty's for a long time. She was losing her eyesight and had difficulty identifying some of the food, so she said to the person in front of her, "Excuse me, can you help me? I can't really see what I am taking." Donna Douglas, the lady in front of Edith, turned around and with a sweet smile said, "Of course, I can help." Edith said, "Thank you, dear, and what is your name?" "I'm Donna," came the simple reply, and she proceeded to help Edith fill her plate with the most delicious goodies. Donna Douglas was truly a shining example of a person who is surrendered to the Lord and can be a servant without getting any applause or fanfare. I happened to be close enough to the exchange to hear what was happening, and it registered in my mind as a lesson to be learned and absorbed in how to be kind and self-effacing. Donna also gave generously of herself to give Trinity Television a character named "Elly" for one of their children's programs. All in all, she was a wonderful blessing.

We had one celebrity who miraculously was able to attend the telethon. Winnipeg was surrounded and covered by a very thick fog, which had all but shut down the airport. The only plane that was allowed to land was the flight from Minneapolis, carrying our main telethon guest, "Mr. White Bucks" himself—Pat Boone. It was one of those "God things" where the fog just sort of opened up enough over the airport to let the flight land. There were a lot of relieved folks around Trinity.

Even Mayor Bill Norrie had to come over to the studio to greet Pat and welcome him to Winnipeg. I mention Pat Boone in the context of my personal experience with Trinity Television not because I was at the telethon that night (I was watching the broadcast from my warm and safe home in Newton), but because of an encounter that I had in the Palm Springs Airport.

Warren and I had gone to a truss industry workshop/conference and decided to take the whole family along since our business partners were taking their entire families. The airline connections were not direct, and we had taken most of the day to travel to Palm Springs. I was tired as well as excited to be in such an exotic place. The children and I were sitting in a group by the luggage carousel waiting for Warren to get the rental car. There was a large pile of matched luggage sitting by the carousel, as if it had been there for a while. I was looking at the luggage and wondering who it belonged to and why it was just sitting there. My eyes swept the nearly empty, tiny airport and I saw a lady walking through the building. For some reason as I looked at her face I thought, "My goodness, that lady's face is just shining with Jesus." I did not know why I thought that, but my next thought was that she looked vaguely familiar, then I saw the man who was walking a little bit behind her and I realized that it was Pat Boone! The lady whose face was glowing with Jesus' love was none other than Shirley Boone. She walked up to the pile of luggage and took charge of it.

Warren came over with the car rental keys to where we were sitting. Before I could point the Boones out to him, he saw them and walked over to Pat Boone, introduced himself, and reminded Pat about being on the Trinity Television tele-thon. Pat was very pleasant and said to say "Hi!" to Willard and Betty and that was that. Years later, I had the feeling that I should have written to Shirley Boone to tell her about that encounter and how that before I knew who she was, I recog-nized the love of the Lord on her face. I think we all need to be encouraged that our light is shining through, no matter who we are!

On that same trip to Palm Springs we had encounter with another Christian broadcaster. One of the other wives and I went to a shopping mall close to the condominium complex where our families were staying. We stopped at the food court and were standing at the yogurt stand waiting to order our fro-zen treats. As we stood there, I glanced to my right and looked straight into the eyes of Tammy Faye Bakker. Silly me stam-mered something stupid like, "Oh, it's you!" I know, totally lame. She was very gracious and replied, "Yes." We chatted for a few minutes and told her we were from Canada on a busi-ness trip with our husbands and families. She was sweet and genuine. My friend and I sat down to visit and enjoy our fro-zen yogurt. Out of the corner of my eye I saw a group of girls suddenly get all giggly and pointing over to where Tammy and her daughter were sitting and having a quiet conversation. The girls went over to their table and made a big fuss as they rudely interrupted them. I felt bad for the intrusion on their private time. The next time I looked, Tammy and her daughter had left the food court. I discovered later that the Bakker family was going through a very traumatic time in their life and ministry. Knowing that made me even more sad that people in the very public ministry of television could not enjoy the simple plea-sure of going to the mall for a quiet visit and ice cream. I was shocked and saddened to find out that Jim Bakker had been put in prison. He later was released, and all the charges against him were dropped. God is good and will never let His people suffer without bringing something positive out of the negative.

In 2007, Tammy went home to be with the Lord. The daughter she had been trying to talk to at the mall has been healed of her wounds and is in ministry with her Dad in Branson, Missouri. Jim has been restored to television ministry and has a vision to see young people trained in television ministry. I think it is really cool that he talks about the NOW generation. God does not let any of His good ideas die without bringing new life. I can't resist mentioning that Lori Bakker, Jim's new wife, contributed to the *Women of Destiny* Bible. Betty Thiessen is also included as a contributor to that special edition of God's Word.

Another event that was ordained by the Lord was the booking of a relatively unknown author who was in the Manitoba area. He had been on tour with the Campus Crusade/ Power To Change ministry. His tour organizers were trying to book him onto *It's a New Day* without any success. A friend of mine who worked in the Power to Change office called me to ask if I could pull some strings. I told her I would see what I could do and called the guest coordinator at *New Day*, who was a gal from the Oakville area whom I had known for years (I had sung at her wedding). Thankfully, it worked out for the author to be interviewed and present his latest book. I was happy to be part of the booking of Joel C. Rosenberg. I actually wrote him a note and asked him to autograph a copy of his book, *The Last Days*, that I gave to my son, David. A funny footnote is that his 2005 book, *The Ezekiel Option*, became the ministry's featured product of the month. It is one of the testimonies of trust and faith that I look at as I am thankful that I am an obedient follower of the Way.

I could go on with my "Name Dropping 101," but I really want to share some of the notable events that have occurred with Trinity Television. I really have some miraculous, "Go-dincidence," happenings that require a bit of building. I need to go back many years in my Christian life in order to set the stage for the amazing story that I want to share with you.

13. Healing Power of Prayer—Part 3

Warren and I are part of the praise and worship group called Power in Praise. The group has gained a certain notoriety in the Winnipeg area, and we are widely known for our ability to lead people to be worshippers in spirit and in truth as we lead them in corporate worship into the heavenly Throne Room of God—the Holy of Holies. A Messianic Jewish pastor in Winnipeg, Moishe Weinberg, called me one day in the mid-1970's —seemingly out of the blue—to ask if I would write a Purim play for his congregation. I did not see myself as a playwright. I was just a little Gospel singer! I didn't know if I could write a whole play, but for some reason known only to the Lord, I accepted the challenge and proceeded to write the Purim play. I did some research by reading the Book of Esther. I wrote the play, gave it to Moishe, and kept a copy for myself. I didn't know if the play was ever performed, but I felt that I had done this as a favor and I put it out of my mind. Years later, I came across the play and God gave me music to enhance the story. I reworked the script and kept it in a drawer, mainly out of sight and out of mind. As songs would come to me over the course of the next few years, I would write them down. I had other songs that I had written and performed on occasion, but for the most part I felt more comfortable doing music written and performed by others. I know that I was learning to expose myself to new experiences in letting go of my fears and inhibitions. I really wanted to be a conduit for the Lord to pour in me and through me whatever He had for me to do.

At that time I was part of a church music committee, and for "some reason" I started telling them about the "Esther musical." They were very excited to have an original play to put on in the church, so I began to put the script together. My biggest struggle was how to arrange the music, because I could not read or write music very well. I truly know that my musical ability comes from the Lord, as I am not formally trained. I taught myself the rudiments of music so that I could put the music that was in my head on paper, but it was a far cry from having arrangements for performance quality rehearsals. For some reason, I had a mental block trying to get the music done. I had the script of the play, but I felt a decided "check" when it came to finishing the product. I don't know if I was being disobedient or if the timing was not right, but either way the project slipped into oblivion.

In the fall of 1999, I was in Edmonton at a wedding when the Lord gently told me that He wanted me to finish the project and give it to Trinity Television. This took place over the Thanksgiving long weekend. I had been privileged to be part of my sister's prayer group. We had watched the faith building video called "Transformations", which is about how God is transforming communities around the world. There is revival occurring in various places and through a variety of circumstances. I was very moved by the different stories, and my faith was built up. I felt a definite clarity and knew that God had a definite purpose for me to share my "Esther" project with the folks at Trinity Television. I knew that I wanted to be obedient, although I did not know what Trinity would do with the property. When I returned home, I prepared the script to take to Trinity.

At that time I had been going through a physical problem that needed to be corrected. The doctor had discovered that my hemoglobin was dangerously low; in fact, the nurses who took my blood were amazed that I was walking, talking, and functioning, because the count was 70 when normal was 130 or higher. So I was a walking miracle! The doctor determined that I needed to have a hysterectomy. I was scheduled to go in for the surgery, and I wanted to make sure that I had everything turned over to Trinity before my surgery day. Somewhere in the back of my mind was the thought that I needed to make sure all of this was done beforehand, because one never knew with surgery if one would wake up from the anesthesia! That was my thinking, so I dropped the "Esther" script off at the Trinity front desk early in November. Betty "just happened" to be standing by the reception desk, and asked me if I would be available to sing "Oh Holy Night" at the "Christmas-In-No-vember-Dessert-and-Coffee" that they were planning to tape on November 25 and 26. My surgery was scheduled for No-vember 24, so I told her that it might not work. Betty said, "Maybe they can postpone it." I could hardly believe the words that came out of my mouth as I heard myself saying, "Maybe God can give me a miracle of healing through it!" I know that those words were not mine; God sort of took over! Betty got really excited and gave me a tape of healing scriptures. The ball really got rolling after that!

God gave me a list of people that He wanted me to share this special request for healing with, as well as a list of specif-ics that we were to pray for. I contacted the people on my list, and we began to believe God that I could receive all the items on my request list. I believe God gave me the prayer people and He gave me the list of prayer items. There was the obvious prayer item of being able to recover enough from the surgery on Wednesday, November 24, to be able to attend the dessert and coffee on Thursday, November 25 or Friday November 26, and to be able to sing "Oh Holy Night." This would have been the definite sign that a miracle had taken place! My understanding of this type of surgery is that ladies need weeks and weeks, if not months, to recuperate, so that item in itself was a huge leap of faith. A hysterectomy is considered major surgery, and I was having my fibroid-laden uterus removed through an abdominal incision. We were to pray that I would have favor with the hospital staff and favor with my gynecologist. I didn't know what that meant, but I was being obedient to the prompting of the Spirit of the Lord. We were to pray that I would not have undue pain or require morphine, and that I would not suffer from the ill effects of the general anesthetic.

One of the people on my prayer list was Joanne, who was the prayer coordinator at that time. I phoned her on November 22, 1999, to agree together over the situation. I've looked back at the little prayer journal that I kept to make sure of the items that we included in our prayer. We prayed that I would not need the self-regulated morphine, that my bowels and bladder would function properly right away, that I would be awake and aware in the O.R., and that I would be up and walking and talking right away. We prayed that I would have favor with the staff and Dr. McGregor, that I would make a difference in the place, and finally that I would be free to attend one of the Christmas Dessert Coffee evenings on the 25 or the 26 of November to sing for the Glory of God! She made me feel like I could walk on water. Her faith and the power of agreement in trusting the Lord brought my faith to a place I never knew I could experience. I wrote in my journal all the things we were asking for by faith. Prior to my sharing with Joanne, I had to go to the St. Boniface Hospital for an information session. The nurse pulled out all kinds of paraphernalia, like catheter tubes and bags. She explained that I would have an "epi-morph", which entailed getting a needle in my spine to deaden the nerves and lessen the pain of the surgery. The thought of getting a needle in my spine sent shock waves of warnings through me. I did not enjoy needles at the best of times, but the idea of a needle in my back was just a little too horrific for me (although my son Peter had fallen asleep during his lumbar puncture!). I asked the nurse if there was some other course of action. She was sort of "by the book," but she said if I really did not want to have the epi-morph then I could have a self-administered morphine IV, but it would also have to be agreed to by the attending anesthetist. That sounded good to me!

My surgery day arrived and my husband took me to the admitting area. He dropped me off and took David over to Trinity Television to be a volunteer camera operator. Warren came back and sat with me until surgery time. Something unusual happened that didn't seem to make sense at the time, but made perfect sense after the surgery. The nurse who met me in the ward said she would start the IV. That seemed like a logical procedure, but when I was taken down to the pre-op area another nurse said that the IV I had received in the ward was not big enough for the volume of fluid that I might require, so they froze my hand and put in a larger bore IV I had two drips, which of course made for a large amount of fluid coursing through my body. The different personnel I encountered were all very efficient and willing to explain any procedures that they were doing. The prep-nurse that wrapped my hair in a towel and put tight leggings on me to prevent blood clots was a gentleman who looked more like a wrestler than a nurse. They finally wheeled me into the O.R. and had me slide onto the narrow table. The operating room nurses introduced themselves, but they were wearing masks, so I really did not know who they were. Dr. MacGregor came in to the operating room.

I felt very wide awake and mentioned that it was so strange to think I was so wide awake and yet in a few minutes I would be so totally asleep! Then they put the rubber gas mask over my face and said to breathe normally. My last thought was wondering who was holding my hand.

The next thing I knew I heard a voice saying, "Your surgery is over, Linda, you can wake up now." I opened my eyes. Warren and David were standing at the foot of the bed, and I had this annoying, pinching feeling that I knew was the catheter. I mentioned that it was annoying a couple of times, but other than that I felt normal. I saw a serious looking IV apparatus with blinking lights by the bed, and the nurse said that I had a button I could press to administer the morphine that was inside the blinking box. I thought to myself that if I needed it, I would probably use it, but I did not really feel any discomfort—except for the catheter, which was very annoying! I was wheeled back to my room, and I thought that it was handy that they had moved my unconscious body from the operating table and put me right into my bed on wheels. Warren and David came and visited for a while, but I knew that Warren had to get back to work, so I decided to relax and take a nap.

The nurses kept coming to check on me and my surgical staples, and to empty my little bag at the end of that annoying catheter. They would ask if I had any discomfort, but I was really not feeling bad at all. I slept and enjoyed the quiet of the day. In the evening my parents came to visit me, and the only time I had a wave of nausea occurred when the nurses turned me from one side to the other. Through the night, the nurses would come in and check my vital signs, my staples, and my bag. I didn't feel unusually bad, so I didn't use the morphine.

In the morning, a nurse said that I would be sitting up and swinging my feet over the side of the bed. She said that I would be getting up to void after they removed the catheter. I was relieved, because up until that point the most annoying thing was the discomfort of the catheter tube. I had felt pinches in one side where the staples were, but nothing that I could not handle. After the nurse took out the catheter, I felt greatly relieved. The next good thing was the removal of the original IV that had been given to me on the ward. Another nurse, Virginia, came in to help me stand up and make my way to the washroom. This same nurse had helped me sit up early in the day, and she had said I could not rely on the usual muscles for a little while. Her actual words were, "You won't be able to do your Jane Fonda moves for a little while!" Virginia said I might need a small dose of morphine, and I was surprised at my inability to stand up straight and at the extra sharp pinching of one of the surgical staples. I pressed the "self-morph" button, which administered 3 mg of morphine into my system. I made my way to the washroom, dragging my IV stand. I took my time and was successful in all of the maneuvers of exercising my own bladder. Hurray! The nurse said I could walk to the nurse's station in a little while with some help.

A little while later the nurse came to accompany me on my walk. We made our way down the hall to the nurses' station, then turned around and walked (me dragging my IV stand) back to my room. I was sitting on the edge of my bed and feeling very wide awake and spry. I wondered if I would be allowed to go for a walk all by myself, so I got up and walked (dragging my friendly IV stand) to the nurses' desk. When I got there I asked if I could walk on my own, and Virginia almost laughed and sort of waved her hand to indicate that it was perfectly all right with her for me to continue walking! It turned out that it was unusual for someone who had just had surgery to be gallivanting through the hospital corridors! I just knew I was feeling great, so I went for a walk, up and down the hallway. I went back to sit in my room for a while.

Later, I received a visit from the pastoral care worker, a lovely lady named Rosalind. I had been listening to the tape that Betty had given me a couple of weeks before with the healing verses of Scripture and piano music accompaniment. Rosalind and I talked about different situations such as mine where healing scripture was so important to build up our faith. She mentioned a personal friend in the hospital who was dying of cancer and asked where she could get that healing tape. I told her about Trinity Television, and said that Betty would probably really want me to pass my copy of the tape to her for her friend. She was very grateful, and I was glad to come alongside and encourage her. We had a lovely visit that was over all too quickly. Eventually, Virginia came in to write a report before her shift was over, and to take out the large bore IV. She removed the needle and began to write and write and write. At one point she looked at me and said, "Do you know that there is a twenty four hour allotment of morphine in this bag? That is 60 mg and you have only used 3 mg?" I just shook my head in amazed wonder and smiled at her. She said something to the effect that I should come back and teach a course on post-operative recovery, but that would mean telling the patients that they would have to ask Jesus to be their Lord and Savior and they would have to listen to healing scriptures and put a list of prayer items together with a list of prayer intercessors. Well, I think that if I was approached to teach a post-operative recovery course it would be a great opportunity to evangelize! I wrote in my journal that I enjoyed the "finding favor with the staff" answer to prayer.

It was Thursday afternoon and I was feeling exceptional. I could have left the hospital that day, but God had His plan perfectly set for me to stay one more night. Earlier in the day, after my last IV was removed, I went for a walk and encountered a lady who was hunched over and walking very slowly. I was coming down the hall toward my room, but I decided to turn around and go back past the nurse's station to the elevators. As I got to the elevator, the lady I had seen a few minutes before stopped me and said, "Excuse me, I just couldn't help but notice you. I know I had my surgery the day before yours, and I can just barely shuffle along. Here you are practically running down the halls. What is your secret?" I was all set to tell her my "secret" when the elevator door popped open and out stepped my mother. I asked the lady her name and what room she was in so that I could stop by and talk to her later and tell her my "secret." She told me her name was Elaine and gave me her room number, and I promised to see her later in the day.

My mom and I walked around, and she was amazed at the difference in me from her visit the previous evening. On the evening of my surgery day, I was full of tubes and had lines of liquid going in and out, so the miraculous transformation as I walked around without any IV stands was pretty dramatic! I was glorifying the Lord, and I could hardly wait to be released from the hospital to go and share my miracle. After my mom left, I went to Elaine's room. I walked in and began to tell her that I was a Christian and about the prayer list, and she almost shouted, "I knew it, I knew it! I knew when I asked you what your secret was and you did not get a chance to tell me. I knew, I knew that you are a Christian!" She was so sweet. We had a lovely chat, but it was cut short when a case worker came in and had to see Elaine. I said goodbye and promised that I would come again to visit with her the next day.

There were other dear people I encountered who reaffirmed to me that God was totally in control. One lady who brought me my meals said that I looked familiar. As we spoke she remembered that I was a singer she had seen on television. At one point she came into my room when I was listening to a song that I was learning for a Christmas concert. She asked if it was me singing on the tape and I told her no, but that by thinking it was me it confirmed to me that I was supposed to sing that particular song for the concert.

My husband brought his mom and dad to visit me on Thursday evening and they were surprised at how well I was doing. I had hoped that they could go to the Thursday evening Christmas dessert, but they just wanted to sit and visit with me. My evening passed very pleasantly, and I was really keen to be released. I had dropped hints to the different personnel that I would like to get a "pass" to go out on Friday night to attend the Trinity Television function.

In the middle of the night I woke up. I was completely wide awake, so I went for a walk down the hallway. At the nurses' station was sitting Bev Stewart, a dear sister in the Lord whom I have known for years. We had a short visit, then I finished my walk down to the elevators and back to my room. I was all by myself in my room, so I turned on the radio. A late night talk show was on, and they were interviewing different Christian ministers about the reality of God and His plans for people's lives. I thought that was pretty much the icing on the cake of my experience, but you can't outdo God's plans. The next morning I had several doctors come and look at me, and I asked if I could please get a pass for a few hours that evening. They were all really impressed with my progress and told me they would let me know. One of the doctors said that I could take a shower, and I was totally thrilled. Virginia came in to my room and gave me directions to the shower room. I thanked her and told her I was off to "jump in the shower." She just laughed out loud and made some comment about my being her model patient. After my shower I headed back to my room, where I was met by a doctor who told me that I was not only able to have a pass, but that I could be released. I was really ecstatic! During the morning another roommate was brought in, a patient who was there for day surgery. I asked her if the tape I was listening to (Handel's *Young Messiah*) was bothering her, and she said that it was actually nice music. We chatted throughout the day. I had to wait for Warren to come and get me at 6:00, so I had lots of time to go around and visit. Late in the afternoon I got into my good clothes. By faith I had packed everything I would need for singing at the Christmas Dessert Coffee. I put on my "singing duds" and my makeup and went to Elaine's room to visit. She had a visitor, her son, but she asked me to stay and tell him about my miracle. We visited until it was time for Elaine's son to leave. He offered to help me carry my suitcase and my potted plant (a gift from my mother) down to the lobby to wait for Warren. It was only 5:30 and Warren was a little bit late, but we made it to Trinity Television by about 7:00.

We saw Betty as we came in and made sure it was still okay for me to sing. She was very encouraging. My daughter and son-in-law's Bible study group had come out to the event. I went over to talk to them, and they were amazed at how I walked as if there was nothing wrong with me. As I was visiting with different people, I saw Bev Stewart, the night nurse. We both hugged and thanked the Lord for His perfect plan. We had dessert, but I was too excited to eat. We had praise and worship and I danced. Then Willard introduced me and I walked up the steps (I could have run). He asked me about the adventure I had just been through. As I was sharing I mentioned that I had seventeen surgical staples in my tummy!

Soon it was time to sing. I hadn't practiced for a week, so I really had to let the Lord "do His Thing" through me. I like the combination of "Jesu Bambino/O Holy Night" because it starts out sort of quiet and builds and builds to a crescendo and then softens again at the end. I knew that I was a little strained, but I was singing for my Jesus and giving glory to my Holy Father for His goodness! When we took on the challenge of looking for a miracle from the Lord, Betty said that if I was able to go through surgery and show up and sing at the Christmas Coffee that she would give me a standing ovation! She was true to her word, bless her heart! Thank you, Jesus! Do you remember I said that Willard had interviewed me briefly before I sang and I mentioned the seventeen surgical staples? Well, the speaker of the evening, Mr. Ken Gaub, whom I have referred to previously, said that when I was hitting the high note that he thought he would have to duck if staples started popping and zinging past his head! I realize that what I experienced through that whole adventure was God's gift to His daughter. As an added bonus to the story, Betty did the introduction to my song on the Christmas special. The story really doesn't end there, mainly because God does not want you to have a "close encounter of the real kind" without giving more opportunities to let Him work through these surrendered houses of clay.

The Sunday before my surgery as we were leaving church and I was shaking hands with the pastor, God impressed on me to tell him about my upcoming surgery, the Trinity Television Christmas Coffee, and the fact that I had a list of intercessors I believed God wanted this gentleman to join. The Sunday after my surgery and the TTI Christmas Dessert Coffee, I was again in church. Ladies were asking Warren, "When is Linda going in for her surgery?" and he would reply "She already had her surgery this week." They could not believe it, even though I was right there in church. In the middle of his message, Pastor Aubrey stopped, looked right at me and said, "Linda!" "Yes, Aubrey?" I replied. He shot back, "Didn't you ask me to pray about something last week? Come up here and tell me about it." I jumped to my feet and ran up the stairs! Don't ya just love it?! Aubrey did a "Willard" type of interview as we talked about my prayer request of the previous week and

God's obvious answer to prayer. Needless to say, some of the ladies in the congregation were still skeptical (sigh). Having eyes they do not see, and ears yet they do not hear. I suppose I could have shown them my scar and had them touch it, but even then would they believe? I can say without reservation that I am thankful for the way the Lord leads us. He does not always give us a clear picture of where we are going, but that is why He is the shepherd and we are the sheep. We hear His voice and follow Him through all the valleys and over all the mountains. Sometimes He does have some interesting ways of unfolding the road map, as I was soon to find out!

14. We Walk by Faith and Not by Sight

I discovered that the actor who portrayed Jesus in the *Visual Bible Series'* episode "Matthew," a gentleman by the name of Bruce Marchiano, was going to be interviewed on *It's a New Day*. I knew that my mother-in-law would love to go and watch the interview live, and I thought, "I can't do a lot of things for my mother in law, but I can do this!" On the day of the interview I took her to Trinity Television. I made sure she was settled into the studio for the interview, then I went to the reception area to chat with Trinity's front desk gal, Loraine. I told her all about my hospital/surgery/singing adventure. She thought that I should write it down.

As I was at the front desk, a brochure caught my eye. It was advertising a cruise to Alaska in September of 2000 with Willard and Betty. On the cruise there would be an "Alpha Study," which examines the question of the meaning of life. At the time I had no reason to want to go on a cruise, let alone an Alaskan cruise. I knew that we had a major trip planned for the summer of 2000 to England, Scotland, and Wales with our friends from Power in Praise, Jim and Marion Cowieson. We had been planning the British trip for quite a while, and I knew our finances were pretty tight for the year. I was in "faith obedience" mode as I picked up the brochure and put it in my pocket. Loraine and I finished our visit, and I made my way back to the studio to collect my mother in law, Grace.

The program was over and Betty was moving some flower arrangements out of the studio to the green room, so I gave her a hand. Willard and Bruce were standing in the green room chatting, so my mother-in-law got to meet with "Jesus." He was very sweet to her and signed her copy of the coffee table book that he had written. I was impressed with his kindness as he chatted with Grace for the few minutes that we were in the Green room. In the car on the way home, she was so thrilled and said, "Wait until I tell the girls at home that I met Jesus!" Of course, she knew that Bruce was simply an actor who played the role Jesus, but she was certainly in her glory. I was happy to give her the opportunity to meet a brother in the Lord who has been privileged to portray our Lord with sensitivity and excellence.

The brochure that I had folded up and put in my pocket was a mystery to me, especially when I got home and put it on my refrigerator! Warren asked me what the brochure was all about and why I was putting it on the refrigerator and why would anyone want to go on an Alaskan cruise and didn't I know that we couldn't afford to think about an Alaskan cruise on top of the major trip we were already taking and…well, you get the gist of what I had to contend with! Whatever God had planned, He was not letting me in on the secret, but I would find out in the fullness of time!!

15. I Have Decided to Follow Jesus— No Turning Back!

The "fullness of time" came. God nudged me in my spirit regarding our business partner's widow, who was also a friend and neighbor. I was to ask her to go on the cruise with me, and I was supposed to take her on the cruise. She was not to pay for anything!

"Hello? Hey, you there! Yes, you—the one with the major miracle in your portfolio! Are you listening? Do I have to repeat myself? Is this thing on?"

"Yes, Lord, I'm listening. Here am I, use me. How come my feet feel like lead and my stomach feels like butterflies and I can't swallow properly and my husband thinks I've gone off the deep end? Hello, Lord? Are you listening? A little illumination would be nice; maybe just a hint that I'm not losing my marbles?"

God really does work in mysterious ways, and He never follows a pattern, which is why we have to walk by faith and not by sight. I could fast forward the year 2000 to the cruise in September, but I have to let you know how the journey toward God's perfect plan unfolded so that you can be encouraged to trust our Leader with your life. I will backtrack just slightly to the day before my surgery. November 23rd , 1999, was unseasonably warm and sunny. I had lots of things to do before I went into the hospital, and one of the things on my list was a quick shopping trip to the grocery store. I was in the store and saw my widowed friend from a distance. I just knew I did not have time to chat with her, and I didn't know that God wanted me to talk to her. Every time I went down an aisle I saw my friend in the distance, and we were on a converging course every single time. After about the fourth time, I started to get the hint that I needed to talk to her, but my natural mind told me I did not have the luxury of time. Silly me. My last resort was to go way over to the other side of the store and then make my way to the checkout stand, almost knocking my friend over in the process! We were in line together, and we walked out to our cars together. She had parked her vehicle right across from mine! As we talked I confessed that I was in a hurry and that I had surgery scheduled for the next day. The little voice in my heart told me to ask her to pray for my miracle. This gracious lady, who had so much of her own pain to deal with, gladly agreed to be part of my list of prayer people. She was the one that God later told me to invite on the Alaskan cruise with Willard and Betty. So now we'll go "back to the future!"

I heard on *It's a New Day* that there would be an information meeting regarding the cruise, so I decided to go. I asked my friend to go with me, but she was unavailable, so my mother-in-law accompanied me. The lady in charge of the information time, Mary Pedersen, was someone I knew from years before when she lived in Winnipeg and had been very involved in Trinity Television. She and her husband, Walter, were now living in Vancouver, and they were helping to plan the cruise. Mary was excited that I was going on the cruise. She basically said "Linda, if you are going on the cruise, maybe you can be part of the music!" I felt so privileged to be asked to minister, but I let her know that I was not sure how I was going to pay for the cruise, even though I definitely felt like God was calling me to take the trip. Needless to say, the thought of being part of the musical ministry team was very interesting to me. Little did I know how amazing and intricate were the different pieces of this mosaic. They would come together to create a beautiful picture of God's loving plans for His children.

16. More "Godincidences"

or

"Neon Signs From Heaven"

When I received the green light from the Lord to proceed with our plans for the cruise, I let Mary know that I would be thrilled to help out in any way I could. Mary was happy to have me on board (sorry for the pun), and we made plans to get together when Mary was in Winnipeg visiting her daughter. Mary and her friend, Stevie (short for Stephanie), came out to my house in Newton for some lunch, and we decided to get together once more while they were in the province. I made a trip into Winnipeg to meet Mary and Stevie and go over some songs. I had a definite feeling that we were to do old standards that everyone would know, like "Amazing Grace" and "How Great Thou Art" and the song that anyone who has ever watched a Billy Graham Crusade would know, "Just As I Am." We sang together in Mary's daughter's kitchen and enjoyed the sweet presence of the Lord as we shared the familiar songs. We sang the songs without accompaniment. Mary had asked me if my friend who was going on the trip would be interested in playing the piano. I was not sure if she would feel up to it, but I will explain that aspect a little later.

I collected my various hymn books and went through them looking for hymns that could be used on the cruise. I knew that we would not be able to get together for a lot of practicing, and even though there were modern praise and worship songs that were familiar to us, we could not be sure that the people we were leading would all know them. Throughout the summer we compared lists and corresponded until we finally agreed on a list of old hymns and some familiar modern choruses.

I had a neat confirmation from the Lord when Jim and Marion and Warren and I were on our trip to Britain. On the Isle of Skye, in a little resort town called Portree, we stumbled upon a Sunday evening service at the local Church of Scotland. It was the strains of "Because He Lives" coming over loud speakers into the town's square that got our attention as we were going for supper. We decided to forgo eating to join our brothers and sisters in their service. What a wonderful time we had, and what a definite and resounding confirmation that the old standard hymns could cross cultural barriers and speak to a diverse crowd of people. That clinched it for me; the standards were the way to go during the Alpha sessions on the cruise.

When I got back from Britain in August, Stevie called me and told me that she was coming to Manitoba. She wanted to get together to finalize the song lists and to sing them into a tape recorder with me. We had the best time together as we praised and worshipped the Lord! We talked at length about her life. She told me that her husband had left her to go and live with another woman, but that he still looked after Stevie and made sure she was comfortable. Stevie had decided that she would honor her marriage vows by not filing for divorce. She was involved with Covenant Keepers, an organization of men and women whose spouses had left them. Members of the group encourage one another to stay true and steadfast and pray for their spouses and reconciliation. I was impressed with this elegant, sweet spirited, genteel lady's faith. I felt a kinship in the Spirit with her by the end of the afternoon. We hugged as she left, and I looked forward to seeing more of my new friend on the cruise.

As I mentioned previously, Mary asked me if my friend could play the piano for the Alpha sessions on the cruise. I did not want to put any undue pressure on her, since she had been so severely wounded by the death of her husband and the subsequent things that occurred in her life; however, I approached her and asked if she would consider playing the piano, but only if she felt up to it. She did not think she would be able to learn new music and didn't want to commit to playing. It was also a painful memory for her, as her husband used to sit on the piano bench while she played. She needed a lot of healing, and she was taking her time and giving herself permission to grieve at her own pace. I knew it was enough for her to go on a trip, so I didn't push things and just left it up to the Lord. Mary, Stevie, and I had been practicing the music a cappella, since they were familiar hymns and we felt fairly comfortable without accompaniment. One day early in the summer, my friend was at my house for coffee and cake, and I mentioned some of the hymns we would be singing on the cruise. She surprised me by responding ,"Oh, Linda, if you are doing hymns, I can certainly handle that!" A miracle—right there in my kitchen! It would be the first of many miraculous events that God had prepared for His kids!

All of the air and cruise tickets had been purchased, and we were moving full speed ahead. We were going to be in Vancouver on Saturday, and Mary had graciously offered to pick us up at the airport and have us stay at her house overnight, since the cruise did not leave until Sunday. We were going to attend a Trinity Television information evening about NOW TV on Saturday evening. The week before the cruise was very busy, and early in the week Mary contacted me to let me know of a slight change in plans. She had several people staying at her house who were arriving earlier in the afternoon. The logistics of getting those folks from the airport back to her house and then returning for us did not seem to be working. She suggested that Stevie pick us up and take us to her house for supper, and we could attend the meeting and stay at Stevie's for the night. This seemed to be the best plan. After this change in plans, which was God's divine appointment and arrangement, we proceeded to prepare for our departure on Saturday for Vancouver.

I have to preface the next part of the story by saying that everything that occurred in getting us to this point was totally orchestrated by the Lord. His fingerprints were all over the events that led up to the cruise and the ministry that took place. If you are reading this and you have any doubts at all that there is a God in Heaven who loves His children and cares about them, then read on and enjoy the adventure that unfolded before us!

In order to set the stage for the events, I have to let you know about one of the activities my friend was involved with a few days before our departure. On Thursday, my friend was attending a memorial golf tournament put on by different business associates of her late husband to honor his memory and raise funds for one of his favorite Christian charities, the Navigators. One of the outstanding qualities of her late husband was his desire to let his love for the Lord shine in his ethical business dealings. Many people were impressed by this integrity, and he would not be afraid to have an answer for anyone who asked about the truth of the Gospel. During supper, she sat next to a supplier who had been a good friend of her late husband's. This supplier had admired her late husband's stand for the Lord and appreciated his life as a born again Christian. Although this man admired the Christian faith of our late friend, he was not ready to accept this life for himself. It is interesting to note that he used the term "born again Christians" to describe those folks that he recognized as having true faith, but he did not seem ready to accept this truth for himself. As he sat next to my friend at supper, he expressed concern for her wellbeing. He asked her how she was and what she was doing, and she mentioned that she was going on an Alaskan cruise in a few days. He brightened considerably and said his cousin's wife was going on an Alaskan cruise in a few days as well.

He kept talking and my friend thought she heard him say, "She's a born again Christian, too. Maybe you will meet her." My friend said, "Those ships are pretty big; I don't think the chances are very good that we'll meet." She left it at that and forgot about the conversation, but the supplier did not forget.

Our departure date arrived and we set out for Vancouver. We had a great flight, and we knew that we would be met at the Vancouver airport by Stevie. I was hoping that in the crush of people I would recognize my new friend. We landed without a problem and went to the designated area to wait. Stevie arrived and hustled us out to her waiting car. She chatted happily with us and apologized that she had been late. She explained that her cousin from Winnipeg was also going on the cruise and that, due to a stroke, was wheelchair-bound. Stevie had been delayed because she was making her cousin comfortable at home prior to picking us up at the airport. It turned out that Stevie's cousin, Elizabeth, was a bright, funny lady who took her infirmity in stride. One of the "Godincidences" was the fact that Elizabeth's husband had passed away about four years previously in much the same fashion as my friend's husband had died. Both men were athletic people who took care of themselves and were fit. They both died of the same mysterious heart condition. Elizabeth's husband had just won a tennis game in a tournament and was in the club house waiting to go into another game when he collapsed and died. My friend's husband was just skating off the ice after his shift of hockey when he fell down on the ice and was gone. Elizabeth had been just as athletic as her husband, but after his death there were several other deaths in the family and Elizabeth suffered the stroke which left her with partial movement in her left leg and a totally lifeless left arm. She was a courageous example of someone who had been through a lot of hard circumstances, yet whose sense of humor was delightful. She had accepted the Lord earlier in the year, so we had the joy of sharing Jesus with our new sister in Christ.

Stevie announced that we would be having a potluck for supper and using up bits and pieces of various items in her refrigerator. We pulled together and got things going in the kitchen. My widowed friend was busy stir frying at the stove. When she went to the fridge to get something, she put her hand on the door handle and froze as she looked at some pictures on the refrigerator door. She exclaimed, "I know those people," and she named the supplier she had encountered at the golf tournament a few days before and his newly married son. Stevie was standing on the other side of the kitchen with a big smile on her face. She told us that her husband's cousin had called her the day before and told her about this friend of his who was a "born again Christian lady" who would be going on an Alaskan cruise. Stevie's first response was the same as my friend's at the golf tournament: "Well, it's a pretty big ship and I don't know if we will encounter one another." When he mentioned that his friend was a widow, however, Stevie asked for her name. He told her and Stevie exclaimed, "She's staying at my house on Saturday night!"

That was pretty exciting, so the supplier suggested that Stevie put the pictures from the wedding up on her fridge. One of the reasons Stevie had come to Manitoba in the summer was to attend this man's son's wedding. That was one of the reasons we were standing by her refrigerator in one of those "God moments" when time seems to stand still. My friend turned to me and said, "Linda, did you know about this?" Well, I didn't, and I was as stunned as she was at the "Godincidence." The great thing about that start to the adventure of the cruise was that it was just the beginning of a big hug from the Father for us kids. Our time on the cruise was so valuable; for me, it was the opportunity to minister to people from different parts of Canada all in one place, and also to meet people on the cruise ship who loved the Lord.

We met one lady, Marilyn Wood, who played piano and sang in one of the lounges. Stevie, Mary, and I were on our way from one part of the ship to another when we paused in the lounge where Marilyn was playing some old show tunes. We stopped at her piano and started to sing along with her. The next thing we knew, she pulled out a travelling microphone and handed it to us. We spent a lot of time singing with Marilyn! Marilyn was a follower of Jesus who told us about life on board the cruise ship. She had fellowship with some of the other entertainers who also loved the Lord, and they would hold regular Bible studies. One of the other entertainers, a tall, charming gentleman named Craig, was interviewed by Willard. It was rather humorous, because we were sitting around the centrum (a large area in the center of the ship that is similar to an atrium) waiting for the dining room doors to open. Craig's trio was just taking a break from their set of pre-dinner music. As we casually conversed, Willard went into interview mode. Someone said that it was too bad there wasn't a camera handy! It really was too bad, because Craig's testimony was very interesting!

When they weren't working, some of the Christian entertainers came to the Alpha sessions. It just proves again how big God's Family is. Hey, isn't that the title of a *Sonshiny Day* tape—*Big, Big, Family*? Why, yes, I believe it is! It was really good to see how people responded to Willard and Betty, even though they did not know what Willard and Betty did for a living. You just can't fake the genuine love and caring of people who have been totally transformed by the love of God. It radiates and touches people's lives no matter where they go or what venue they find themselves in. It was a clear confirmation to me that Willard and Betty were fulfilling the perfect plan and destiny of their lives that the Father had for them from before they were born. Psalm 139:13-18 says that God sees us from the moment of our conception (before I had a brain I was uniquely "Me!"), and He begins to knit us together (our DNA house of clay) before we are born. He also starts writing down in His book of our life all the good things He has planned for us. He is thinking about us! Jeremiah 29:11 says, *"For I know the thoughts that I think toward you, says the Lord, thoughts of peace and not of evil, to give you a future and a hope."* (NKJV) I knew that I was right where God wanted me to be, and that He had put me in that situation for a purpose.

Mary, Stevie, and I were knit together as the song leaders for the Alpha study session, and we had a good time singing show tunes and popular tunes with Marilyn Wood at the little piano lounge. We were having a lovely time of fellowship and just plain fun! One thing that I take very seriously about my singing ability is that I know it is a gift from the Lord. I know that I am to use it for His glory and never my own gain. With that in mind, I am very careful about the use of my gift, so when one of the girls suggested that I enter the ship's talent contest, I just recoiled! My gift was not to be used for a talent contest. Then the Lord spoke into my heart and basically told me that He wanted me to use the gift He had given to show these cruising folks what His generous gifts look like. Mary,

Stevie, and I entered the talent contest, and we also went to Karaoke Night and called ourselves "The Alpha Chicks." It was great fun! When we entered the talent night we used the same name, and we did a medley of songs, specifically some of the alto solos from various Rogers and Hammerstein musicals. We finished the medley with a song called "You'll Never Walk Alone," which carries the message that there is someone out there who wants a relationship with you and loves you and will be with you through every storm in your life. God basically had the last word in the talent night, and we were able to be His messengers.

He also got the last word in the piano lounge with Marilyn. The piano lady, as Marilyn was called, let us be part of her evenings in the lounge, and on the last night of the cruise we joined her for the last song of the evening, Stevie suggested that we sing "The Lord's Prayer." Marilyn agreed and announced it to the listeners. She prefaced her remarks by saying that this was extremely unusual for a lounge number, but we were going to sing it to finish the evening. We sang and people were crying. It just proves once again that people are hungry for the Lord! We had an amazing time of ministry and healing on that trip. The Lord faithfully led my widowed friend further along the path of mending her broken heart, and we even had the proverbial "icing on the cake" finish to the trip.

Stevie's cousin, Elizabeth, had been a great travelling companion with her wonderful joy and sense of humor. Her ability to "whip around" in her wheel chair was really something to see! When we left the cruise ship, we caught a ride to the airport with Stevie and Elizabeth. When we got to the airport we stayed with Elizabeth, who was returning to Winnipeg on the same flight as us. Due to a slight miscommunication with our travel papers, we did not know that we were supposed to confirm our seats when we arrived at the terminal. To make a long story longer, we were given seats quite far down in the airplane, and Elizabeth pointed out to the ticket agent that she could not go that far down the plane's aisle. She was reassigned to First Class and so were my widowed friend and I because we were travelling with Elizabeth. The flight was overbooked, so Willard and Betty and two other cruise people were put on standby. The prospects of getting on the flight did not look good for them, and as we sat in First Class waiting for the plane to finish loading we talked about the miracles we had enjoyed. Elizabeth said, "You know, it would be the neatest miracle for Willard and Betty and the others to get on this flight, too!" The words were no sooner out of her mouth and we heard this very recognizable laugh coming from the jet way. You guessed it! Willard and Betty came on board the plane along with the other two people! During the flight, I sat next to a gentleman who was a member of the organization "Manitobans with Disablities"; we had a great conversation. I found out that he had been on the Trinity Television program *Light Talk*, so he was very familiar with the Christian Media Center and Trinity's ministry.

There had been other programs produced by Trinity Television that God used to help us focus on how large His Kingdom is and how He loves us enough to be involved in every facet of our walk. One part of *It's a New Day* was the segment called the "World and Prayer Focus." During that portion, Greg Mussellman would relate news items from around the world that directly affect the Body of Christ. For the other portion of that segment, Betty would direct our prayer focus to a specific area of the world; for example, we prayed through Canada province by province. These were powerful tools for informing the Church of problems to be lifted up before the throne, as well as for offering praise for what God was doing around the world to effectively change people's lives.

The news section of "World and Prayer Focus" had a fore-runner program called "Kingdom Report." There was a certain news item on "Kingdom Report" that really caught my atten-tion. The item had to do with a family that was going to Ec-uador to begin a ministry to children. The significance of this particular item was the number of people in the family—ten! I saw the segment and I realized that I had met these people before when they were a family of five. In September of 1981, I received a phone call from an elderly lady in our church in Portage. She said something about a family needing clothing or something. It was not very clear what they needed exactly, but could I go to the pastor's house and see about helping these people? Even though she was a little fuzzy on the details, I had an impression that I needed to hop in the car and go to the pastor's home.

When I entered his house, I met Ron and Glenda Allen and their three children. They looked a little tired, and they were trying to keep their children from being too rowdy. Our pastor was a newlywed, so his house was pretty sterile and not child proof at all. His new wife had been in the kitchen for an hour trying to make hot chocolate! I found out that the Allen's were having car trouble, so they had pulled into a place where there was a phone booth and had called the nearest "fami-ly," or church, in the yellow pages. They were en route to the Youth With a Mission Training School in Ontario, all the way from British Columbia. They seemed to be pretty frazzled, so I suggested that they follow me in their car to Newton, and we would put them up until repairs could be done. We slow-ly made our way back home with many stops so Ron could adjust the makeshift belt that was keeping the engine going without overheating.

We got home and the Allan's ended up staying with us for a couple of weeks. Ron worked for Manufab for eight days, and Glenda and I had a great time of fellowship. They performed their puppet show for our Bible study group, and we even got to participate! We had them share with our church and we helped them out financially so they could make their way to school. It is certainly amazing to see how the Lord orchestrates events, draws people together, and through it all makes our paths straight.

Our adventure continued as Trinity Television expanded with NOW TV in Vancouver and more applications being made for a possible NOW TV in the Winnipeg market. I just have to relate the adventures of our trip to Vancouver in August, 2001, to launch "NOW TV." In order to prepare for the premier airing of the new station, some board members were invited to go to Vancouver to help get everything ready for the dedication of the new studios. Warren and I took the time to go out to Vancouver to help. We landed in Vancouver and were picked up at the airport by one of the new sales team members, Alan. We talked about the Lord and the exciting possibilities of airing this innovative, family oriented, faith-based programming. When we arrived at the hotel, which was right next door to the studios of NOW TV, we were quickly put into work mode. We stowed our gear and headed to the studio. Ernie Thiessen (Willard's talented set designer brother) and his wife, Debbie, were busy painting and preparing sets. Warren was given a job and I was handed the keys to a truck to go and pick up some items at the local lumber yard.

One of the other board member's wives, Heidi, got into the truck with me and we ventured out to find the requested items. I just sort of took the keys, the directions, and the shopping list and got the job done! Heidi and I had never been to that section of Vancouver, let alone ever driven in that area. We literally hit the ground running as we carried out our assigned duties. We helped with the painting, building, and fetching jobs that were needed to get the facilities ready for the dedication and open house. We met some amazingly talented people who also love the Lord. Warren and I had taken a lunch break and we were at a table across from a couple who turned out to be Larry and Nancy Meyers. Nancy Stafford Meyers is an actress who is noted for her role in the Andy Griffith show, *Matlock*.

Both Larry and Nancy were dear people who desired to see the media used to spread the message of hope found in Jesus. Through the course of the weekend, we saw the genuine love of the Lord displayed in these sweet servants. We also met Ken and Susan Wales. Susan is an author who has been on *It's a New Day*. Ken is known for his production of Catherine Marshall's novel *Christy*. Warren and Ken hit it off really well, since Ken is passionate about the *Christy* series and Warren is an avid fan of the video series, which we have in our home library. One of Warren's projects that weekend was to construct pillars that would hold television monitors. The eight foot tall black tubes had cut out sections with shelves in them to hold the screens. The display that Warren and Ken created for the *Christy* videos was fairly professional and eye catching.

NOW TV had some great staff, such as Laura Lyn Tyler, who now works for the *700 Club Canada Edition*, Leland Klassen, the clean stand-up comedian who hosted Retro, and Doug Kooy, who hosted various news analysis programs with NOW TV. We were acquainted with Doug Kooy from past ministry with Power in Praise. We had been the special music at one of Doug's speaking events that had been coordinated by our mutual friends, Brent and Donna (the same Donna who hugged me at the Fifth Anniversary Banquet.) Leland also hosted the "Comedy Street" series produced by Trinity Television. He continued to perform his brand of clean comedy through his work at Crossroads Television, Popcorn TV, Laughopolis,

Comedy Channel, and his comedy tournaments. The need for quality, life changing programming was becoming more and more apparent. We really didn't know what the future held, but God knew what would happen within a few short days of the dedication when September 11th took place with all of its worldview changing impact.

While we were in Surrey for the NOW TV premier, we took the time to meet with one of our truss engineering suppliers. This gentleman was a Sunni Muslim, and we had a really good time with him as we asked him about his faith perspective. It was interesting to have so many deep faith topics being broached as we spent a day with this man. At one point he mentioned how much territory we had covered in our discussions about faith, family and work. We didn't know why we had covered the topics that we did until after the events of September 11th, which occurred a few days after we returned home. After that historic, tragic event we discovered that the horrific deeds of a few deluded terrorists affected innocent people worldwide. Our business associate found it more difficult to fly, as he was profiled as a possible threat. Our hearts were grieved by the fear that had suddenly gripped society, but we also saw it as a wakeup call to repentance and looking to God for His comfort and peace. The need for life-affirming television seemed very timely, indeed.

We had an amazing Sunday morning service in the NOW TV studio. Some staff and board members and guests joined together to worship the Lord and receive a teaching/exhortation from Bob Meisner. Bob spoke from his heart as only a wounded warrior could and gave the exhortation to not be like the fearful spies who came back from the land of Canaan with the report of giants in the land who looked at them like they were grasshoppers. Instead, we were to be like Joshua and Caleb, who came back with the report of the land flowing with milk and honey and huge crops of produce. We were to also not be apathetic in our walk of faith, but dynamic (from the Greek word dounamis, which means powerful and explosive, like dynamite.) When one speaks of "explosion," it is usually to describe a destructive force that decimates. In the Kingdom of God, however, we see the death of a seed much like an explosion. When the seed falls into the ground and dies, new life within bursts forth.

The explosion in the Spirit that Trinity Television had experienced through the years had always been like the seed being sown, exploding into new life and bringing forth an increased yield. Willard and Betty's dream for daily Christian television was sown in the Canadian broadcasting ground. Their vision had to die so that others could be birthed.

During the next few years, the pressure of mounting finances and unseen forces leveled against the fledgling television network became very great. We were aware of some of the behind-the-scenes activities and continued to support the people we had grown to love and cherish through the years. NOW TV was birthed by faith, but all things have a season. NOW TV's end was like the seed being planted; it died, but a sweet resurrection would occur to sweeten the bitterness of its death. I had a very interesting vision during a prayer time that I was part of with Betty, Audrey, and Gloria (Jeff's wife). We would meet in the prayer room at the Media Centre and pray over the specific needs of the ministry. During one of our sessions, I had a clear picture of a field with a row of combines taking off the grain. I shared with the ladies that I felt that God was saying that New Day Ministries was one of those combines going out into the harvest field side by side with other television ministries. It was a powerful picture, and I kept thinking about the faithfulness of the Lord to use mere human beings to fulfill His purposes.

Years later, a ministry that we supported had a literal *Guinness World Book of Records* event—the largest number of combines taking off a crop in the shortest amount of time. The friend from the Power to Change office was now involved with the ministry that sponsored this event. It was interesting to me that I had that picture in my head years before. It does not just pertain to television ministry; all ministries are working in the Father's field. It is an exciting time to live as we witness the unprecedented ability to literally go into all the world and preach the Gospel. Willard and Betty officially retired from the ministry they had founded and the Thirty-Fifth Anniversary Banquet was a celebration of what had been built and what was being birthed.

It's a New Day was going to become *My New Day*, piloted by Bob and Audrey Meisner. The Christian Media Centre was sold to another arm of the Body of Christ and the proceeds covered the debts that had been incurred through the years. Sadly, the separation of many fine employees from their job drew a measure of grief, but when there is weeping in the night, joy comes with the morning. There is a confidence in serving the Lord that when He makes a change; it may hurt for a while, but ultimately the change is always for the better for everyone concerned. The Meisner leadership gave them the right to take on the challenge of carrying the ministry in the way that seemed to better serve their vision going forward. We have retained our membership in New Day Ministries, but felt that the Board should be filled with younger folk with a fresh vision for the ministry and so we stepped out of the board position, grateful that we had served and been used to further the work. We were given a lovely clock and a collage of pictures depicting our various times of ministry with the folks at *It's a New Day*.

One of our final "official" engagements with New Day Ministries was the Thirty-Fifth Anniversary Banquet, which was a celebration and a retirement party for Willard and Betty as they passed the baton of leadership to Bob and Audrey. Power in Praise was privileged to sing "My Tribute" by Andre Crouch. It is good to know that we can point to the Lord as the one who deserves all the glory. We were treated to a walk down memory lane by various people who shared the impact of TTI on their lives. I was blessed and humbled to see the evidence of so many years of faithful service.

As one looks at the television landscape of today, there are both the sacred and the profane sharing the airwaves, much like the wheat and the tares. God has raised up networks that are dedicated to sharing His message of hope and eternal life with Him through His Son. There has been a Christian witness on television for many years through local and national voices.

My role with Trinity Television was small in the grand scheme of things, yet I knew that God had written the script of my life and had designed a good chunk of my life to flow together with Trinity Television's ministry. I pray that I can continue to be part of the exciting journey of supporting Christian television and other worthwhile, benevolent endeavors, until the day that I am either sown into the ground or called by Jesus as part of His Church into the home that He has been working on for two thousand years.

My prayer for you, as you have journeyed with me and Trinity Television, is that you will seek the Lord for yourself and establish your own relationship with Him in the adventure of His kingdom life. If you don't know Him, He is patiently waiting to be your Lord and Savior; all you have to do is ask Him to come into your heart and your life and make you a child of our Heavenly Father. His forgiveness is free, because He paid the debt of your separation from God by His own finished sacrifice on Calvary, and His blood cleanses us from all unrighteousness. The verse of Scripture that Jesus read in the synagogue so many years ago is the truth. In Luke 4 He reads Isaiah 61:

> "The Spirit of the Lord is upon Me, because he has anointed me to proclaim good news to the poor; He has sent me to proclaim liberty to the captives and recovering of sight to the blind, to set at liberty those who are oppressed, to proclaim the year of the Lord's favour." And he rolled up the scroll and gave it back to the attendant and sat down...and he began to say to them, "Today this Scripture has been fulfilled in your hearing." (Luke 4:18-21)

Rejoice and be glad! If you call on the Lord, then the promise is true for you. Today is the day of salvation! It doesn't get much better than that!

Epilogue

To end this story is not possible, because God is forever moving and working and designing our lives and leading us in His paths of righteousness. My own story with the Lord, who plants the seed and ideas like Trinity Television into open hearts like Willard and Betty's, will continue as long as God gives me breath and life in this world and life in the world to come. I have been so very blessed to be part of a television ministry that can go where we are not able to go and be available when we cannot be available. I had an eye opening view of an untapped mission field when I went in to see a dear friend lying comatose in the Deer Lodge Center. I felt led to go and pray at her bedside. As I was standing by her side, her husband came into the room to take her for a walk in her wheelchair. The people on that ward were, for the most part, comatose. I had explained to him that when I first went into her room, the T.V. was tuned to a rude program, so I turned it off. It was distressing for him to know that garbage television was on, since he had left explicit instructions that only educational television was to be on in her room. The other people on the ward each had a television, and the staff would just come in and turn on the T.V. for stimulation. God spoke firmly into my heart that these people needed to be exposed to life changing television, life giving television, truth telling television. I knew I was to be part of the plan to see that this mission field of people, who had impaired bodies and minds but whose spirits were still intact, eternal, and ready to receive Living Water, could be exposed to the Gospel of Jesus through the powerful tool of Christian television.

The ministry continues to go out over the airwaves. There is still music being played that will bring peace and healing to the soul of any who tune in to hear and receive. I was encouraged when I turned on a program called *Time To Sing*, hosted by a lady who I knew from the early days when she would sing with her sister on *It's a New Day*. As I watched the program, which featured a group of people sitting in the choir loft of a church and singing the old hymns, I recognized several people, apart from the host, who had contributed to the music of *It's a New Day*. The flow of life giving television continues through the witness of individual programs, such as *My New Day*, and networks such as Crossroads Christian Television, Grace TV, The Miracle Channel, Vision TV, and so many other networks and programs produced by God's people. It can reach into the hospitals, the houses of seniors and young people, the homes that are filled with conflict and pain, and the devices of people from all walks of life and economic status, and bring the hope of Life for today and on into eternity. We can do our part by prayerfully and financially supporting the work as the Lord leads. I am ready to continue to do my part—are you?

About the Author

Born in 1952 in Winnipeg, Manitoba, Linda was the second child in a family of four girls and two boys. She had a typical Canadian upbringing, which included being exposed to the Christian message through reading the Bible in school, attending Sunday School, and celebrating the Christian holidays of Christmas and Easter.

In 1970, at the age of eighteen, she turned the head knowledge of knowing about Christ into the heart knowledge of accepting Christ's redemptive gift of eternal life when she accepted Jesus as her own, personal Saviour and Lord.

She married her high school sweetheart, Warren, in 1973, and has enjoyed a lifetime of adventures with him. They have three married children and four grandchildren.

Music, ministry, and miracles have been a large part of Linda's life. Her initial appearance in 1977 on *It's a New Day* led to more appearances on television, as well as behind the scenes activities with the ministry of Trinity Television. Linda feels privileged to have been an eyewitness to a piece of history known as Christian television in Canada.

In sharing her story, she hopes that others will be encouraged and challenged to support this unique tool of sowing, reaping, and harvesting in the King's fields.